The Scientific Case Against
Scientific Creationism

The Scientific Case Against Scientific Creationism

Jon P. Alston

iUniverse, Inc.
New York Lincoln Shanghai

The Scientific Case Against Scientific Creationism

iUniverse, Inc.

For information address:
iUniverse, Inc.
2021 Pine Lake Road, Suite 100
Lincoln, NE 68512
www.iuniverse.com

ISBN: 0-595-29108-2

Printed in the United States of America

To John Boies, Ruth Larson, Harland Prechel, and Laurie Silver, who fought
    honorably against malevolent colleagues and hostile university administra-
    tors.

To Margaret Alston and Greg Goodwin, and Susan Lewis Phariss and Paul
    Phariss, who are enjoying new beginnings in their lives.

To Bruce Dickson and Dick Startzman, valued friends and colleagues.

To my wife, Letitia, who should also be writing books instead of helping others.

To those who helped me find my way in a new discipline and encouraged my
    efforts, including Hal Hall, Andrew J. Petto, and John Wickham.

Contents

Introduction

o o o o o o o o o o o o o o o o o o o o o o o o o o o o o o o o o o
Nothing in biology makes sense except in the light of evolution.

—*Theodosius Dobzhansky*

Why This Book Was Written

The idea for yet another book criticizing scientific creationism and creationists' attacks on evolution originated from a newspaper report of high school science teacher Rodney LeVake. LeVake refused to teach evolution as part of his class's biology curriculum and he wanted to show the students the errors in their biology textbook falsely supporting evolution. LeVake claimed he did so because his religious beliefs and self-studies convinced him evolution, as proposed by Charles Darwin and supporters, is false and creationism true in a scientific sense. LeVake did not mention his beliefs included more than criticisms of evolution. The beliefs underlying LeVake's mindset also forced him to believe in a worldwide flood, a literal six days of creation, and other beliefs that orthodox scientists have found to be completely without proof and foundation. This book describes and evaluates these beliefs to show the irrational consequences of beliefs based on scientific creationism. I show that the alleged "science" in scientific creationism is without proof and made up of "just-so" stories developed to defend religious beliefs. Scientific creationism is a religious wolf wearing a pseudo-scientific fleece. Although Rod LeVake believed evolution should not be part of a science curriculum, evolutionary theory is in fact based on a massive amount of observations, measurements, and field studies conducted during the last 150 years.

I wrote this book to show LeVake, his students, and co-religionists that scientific creationism is not true science and that its criticisms of evolution are false and non-scientific. Scientific creationism, with its supernatural elements, cannot replace empirical science without damaging the educational process. Evolution remains the best description of the development of life and of the variety of organisms including plants, animals, and humans than any other models.

1

Scientific creationism is a pseudo-science based on religious rather than empirical foundations. Scientific creationists believe the first eleven chapters of the book of Genesis offer explanations and descriptions of the world and biological diversity that are empirical (i.e., objective). They wish to include these religious beliefs as part of the educational process. Orthodox scientists and the legal courts find scientific creationism is a religious worldview ultimately unsupported by empirical methods. I strongly oppose the claims of scientific creationists that their religious beliefs are as scientific as evolutionary theories. This book was written to show scientific creationism is a false science and does not offer new understanding in the study of life. Scientific creationism is associated with religiously based beliefs that have no validity. I will show that acceptance of scientific creationism also necessitates the acceptance of beliefs in numerous impossibilities based on the scientific creationists' selective interpretations of Biblical passages.

An example of the relative utility of evolutionary and creationist explanations is found in the distribution of chipmunks species. There are twenty-two different species of chipmunks in the United States (Hall, 1981). However, one is located in the east while twenty-one species are found in the west (Brand, 1997: 1). Evolutionists would predict more species exist in the west because there are more varied habitats in the west forcing isolated populations of chipmunks to evolve into different species to better survive in different ecological niches. By contrast, scientific creationists explain the different dispersion of chipmunk species as God's will, that they traveled to their current homes by themselves, or that one of Noah's descendants took chipmunks from Turkey to North America and left them in various places. The evolutionary model allows researchers to predict different species will be found in different habitats and that uniform environments will contain fewer species, as is in fact found in the eastern United States.

There is no demand currently to place a "creationist grammar" or "creationist art" (that may come later) in public school curricula. Yet evolutionists and those who teach evolution are censured and harassed by scientific creationists. Supporters of evolution, and I am one, need to convince others how unscientific and dangerous to the educational process is scientific creationism.

Scientific Creationism vs. Evolution

This book presents the major arguments of scientific creationists. Creationists believe God created the universe and all life as described in the book of Genesis in the Jewish Bible. In addition, scientific creationists believe the creationist account of the origin and diversity of life is not only correct but is also as scientific and factual as evolutionary theory. They argue scientific principles support their Biblical beliefs and the supernatural is a central element in the development of life and its diversity. By contrast, evolutionists believe life evolved and developed on earth over a great length of time through natural processes first systematically proposed by Charles Darwin. While evolutionists disagree among themselves how evolutionary changes are brought about, all would agree the structure and behavior of current life are best understood in terms of natural forces such as adaptation to environmental changes, competition for resources, and mutation. There is no need to include the supernatural to explain the diversity of life.

Scientific creationists ignore a basic element in science: science prospers and develops through disagreement. Scientists defend their positions and criticize others' positions and test which view of the topic is better. Criticism of one part of evolution does not destroy the whole edifice of evolutionary knowledge; it instead encourages the search for additional knowledge and the integration of disparate positions. Science advances through the discovery of information disagreeing with or absent from established knowledge. Scientists either reformulate their theories or discard them when new information compellingly questions established knowledge.

By contrast, scientific creationists refuse to question their religiously based knowledge; they are forced to fit facts into their preconceived Biblically based frameworks and ignore data contradicting their beliefs. As a result, scientific creationism cannot be integrated into secular science without damaging the teaching of science. Scientific creationists' attacks on established science is a serious and unwarranted insertion of religion into science in public school curricula. This book was written to show contemporary creationism in its many forms is false science and an irrational use of scientific principles (Kitcher, 1982: 171).

Scientific creationists cannot reinterpret their religious sources (Berra, 1990: 108), which is why religious knowledge is stable and does not accumulate in the way science accumulates knowledge and discards data that have been disproved. Scientists, in the long run, discard their errors and accumulate supported and valid findings. Scientific creationists focus their attention on finding ambiguities in evolutionary findings but cannot correct them or suggest explanations other than those found in Biblical scripture. Often using evolutionists' own criticism of one another, scientific creationists assume factual errors can bring evolution into doubt and be discarded. By contrast, scientists see inconsistencies in their theories not as disproof but rather as opportunities to refine established knowledge.

All but the most recalcitrant religionists accept the fact evolution *has* taken place. There are too many collections of fossils and the results of too many field and laboratory studies to ignore the fact changes in organisms have taken place over a long period. It is still unclear *how* evolutionary changes have taken place and there remain many ambiguities in the understanding of the processes of evolution. The statement by Simon Conway Morris (1998: 10) "that evolution is rich in unsolved problems is not in dispute" acknowledges there is much to be discovered in the areas of evolution. However, lack of knowledge does not mean that evolution is false as the scientific creationists hold. What is known, however, is reliable and explains biological diversity better than any other competing system of thought, including the one found in the first chapters of the book of Genesis.

What this Book Accomplishes

I quote extensively from scientific creationists' writing to show exactly what they say. Too many critics of scientific creationists ignore their writings of a theological character while focusing their criticisms on what scientific creationists say about evolution. However, scientific creationists should be held responsible not only for what they say about evolution, but also for their religious arguments. This book critically analyzes scientific creationism and the accompanied theological beliefs rather than evolution *per se*. The evaluation of the works of Darwinians, neo-Darwinians, and other evolutionists is a task for others and for other books. The major rationale of scientific creationists for their work is criticizing evolutionary theories with the assumption doing so validates their own worldview and religious beliefs. I show that these scientific creationist views are not acceptable as possible topics in educational curricula, nor are they scientifically acceptable. That is why I devote a chapter each to the Noachian flood and its aftermath. Those who accept scientific creationism accept a wide range of theological and secular beliefs that are counter to common sense and scientific knowledge.

My approach toward the analysis of scientific creationism is in the same spirit Richard Miller (1987) recommends for an analysis of conflicting ideologies or competing scientific models. Miller proposes rival theoretical approaches be evaluated by using the best of each framework. By contrast, the practice in law courts is to ignore the best evidence of one's opponent and to present only one's own best case. Science is different. Scientists are obliged to represent the case of rival theories as fully as possible in a way that would be acceptable to their opposites. I will present the "best cases" for scientific creationism and analyze them to see if they are valid from an orthodox scientific perspective.

Comparisons of scientific creationism with evolution show it has little if any scientific validity and evolution proves superior whenever creationists make statements that are empirically testable. I have no quarrel with statements based on religious scriptures unless they deal with testable statements contradicting accepted knowledge.

Scientific creationists believe the Bible is as scientific as any secular textbook (Morris and Morris, 1996 and Morris, 1977b). Moreover, scientific creationists declare the scriptures must be accepted when a conflict exists between science and the scriptures. This position forces scientific creationists to defend their interpretation of scripture in increasingly convoluted ways in the face of conflicting evidence. I present these aberrations from established knowledge in the chapters that follow. These differences between scientific knowledge and Biblical interpretation challenge the religiously derived statements of the scientific creationists. Scientists should test all empirical statements made by scientific creationists; when they are in conflict, the religious statements will be found to be false.

Orthodox science has limits creationists use to their advantage. Science deals with only the material, measurable world (Eldredge, 2000: 137). Scientists develop generalizations from their observations of nature, from theories, or even from educated guesses. Eventually, however, generalizations and causal models are tested to see if they have any validity. Creationists do not test their basic assumptions because doing so would result in questioning their religious faith.

Scientific creationists such as Phillip Johnson ridicule the notion scientific naturalism has any validity when it differs from Biblical passages. The response of orthodox scientists is that science is not and cannot include the supernatural in its deliberations. By contrast, scientific creationists include the supernatural in their discussions and their causal models. This is the major difference between the two worldviews: evolutionists reject the supernatural element as a part of science while scientific creationists insist that all deliberations take into account Biblical scriptures. To use the title of a book by evolutionist Gary Cziko (1995), the naturalistic scientific approach searches to understand the world "without miracles" and has no interest in attacking religious statements *unless they are empirical in character.*

The Limited Character of Scientific Creationism

Scientific creationists have yet to present research validating their theological positions while at the same time denying established findings contradicting their theology. I take issue with scientific creationists such as Roger DeHart, a high school science teacher similar to Rod LeVake (Savoye, 2000). DeHart teaches evolution as part of his duties. DeHart also discusses during the last day of the evolution module the topic of intelligent design, a contemporary form of scientific creationism (see chapter seven). Intelligent design proponents focus on the proposition that organisms are too complicated to have evolved without a creator/designer. DeHart's defense was that he did not mention religious beliefs, but offered intelligent design as an alternative to evolution processes. We see here an attempt to introduce religiously based material into the classroom under the disguise of impartiality.

By the same token, statements by scientists dealing with such questions as ultimate meanings, issues of good and bad, or the supernatural are just as inappropriate. Stephen Jay Gould has shown the disastrous consequences when science includes religious and political biases or is used to support ideological biases. In his book *The Mismeasure of Man* (1981: chapter seven), Gould admits that, while racism was prevalent before Darwin's theory of evolution was introduced, later ideologists used the evolutionary framework to support their own prejudices (see also Ruse, 1998, 1999, and 2003). Such prejudices have no place in evolutionary thought today and have been thoroughly discredited. Science is at its best when it does not contain external biases, including those of self-aggrandizement, social interests, or of a religious nature.

Robert T. Pennock (1999) states there is only one valid science; it must be naturalistic and seek only natural laws and causes. It is for this reason that science is universal and it makes no sense to talk about a "Hindu science," a "Roman Catholic science," or a "left-handed people science." Scientific creationism, with its reliance on the supernatural and on interpretations based on their unique religious views, violates the scientific axiom that scientists seek natural causes and explanations apart from all religious frameworks. Science should also operate outside personal biases and political ideologies. Errors in knowledge occur when scientists do not follow these ideals, as when T.D. Lysenko imposed his anti-evolutionary ideological views on Russian genetic studies and, as a result, destroyed Russian agricultural sciences for a generation.

Charles Robert Darwin (1809–1882) noted the use of religious explanations was a lazy way of seeking knowledge because it is easy to claim an event was caused by a miracle and therefore needs no further explanation. Science, with its emphasis on dealing with the observable world, is more effective than other sources of knowledge in solving practical problems. We no longer assume that rain and lighting are caused by angry gods; using non-supernatural investigations, we can now better understand and predict tomorrow's weather.

There is a tendency among both evolutionists and creationists to ridicule and denigrate their opposites. Evolutionist Richard Dawkins (1989: 35) denounces creationists as ignorant:

> It is absolutely safe to say that if you meet somebody who claims not to believe in evolution, that person is ignorant, stupid or insane (or wicked, but I'd rather not consider that)...[This is] an area where half the country claims to believe an absurd and palpable falsehood. I say "claims" because a belief that is held in carefully nurtured ignorance of the alternative is hardly a belief to be taken seriously.

The above statement is extreme but understandable from a strictly non-theistic, partisan evolutionist perspective. Many statements made by scientific creationists have repeatedly been shown to be false by well-established evidence. Furthermore, scientific creationists ignore valid evidence disagreeing with their beliefs while they misinterpret scientific statements when it suits their purposes. Nevertheless, much of the anti-evolutionary work of scientific creationists forms a cohesive whole based on rigorous analysis within a religious framework. I present creationists' major statements and evaluate their validity in terms of empirical, non-religious standards. I reject the charge that scientific creationists are "ignorant" or "stupid." If that were true, scientific creationism would have disappeared long ago as a serious challenge to evolutionary theories. Scientific creationism is based on decades of analysis and study and should not be dismissed in a cavalier manner. On the other hand, the statements of scientific creationists should be respectfully challenged whenever appropriate.

The works of scientific creationists show their religious contexts and I quote extensively from major creationists to show their non-empirical biases. Few persons are aware an acceptance of scientific creationism leads to other positions that from an empirical perspective are irrational and unbelievable. That is why I analyze in detail what scientific creationists write concerning the Noachian flood, the ark, and the alleged repopulation and distribution of the world's animals.

Preview of Chapters

Each chapter in this book presents a different aspect of the creationist ideology. I discuss in the first chapter the different forms of creationism. Creationism consists of a number of different positions and arguments although one form, scientific creationism, is currently dominant. Another form of the creationist argument, intelligent design, resembles scientific creationism but offers different emphases.

The second chapter presents three major creationist-evolution confrontations: the 1860 Huxley-Wilberforce debate, the 1925 John Scopes trial, better known as the "monkey trial," and the 1968 *Epperson* v. *Arkansas* case presented before the U. S. Supreme Court. Each confrontation delimits a distinct strategy of scientific creationists and, for the last two cases, a definition of the legal standing of creationism *vis à vis* public schools. Creationists are adaptable and they continuously develop new rhetorical (though not new evidence) strategies to promote their cause. Evolutionists by contrast have maintained relatively stable responses to scientific creationism during the last seventy-five years or even since Charles Darwin published his *The Origin of the Species by Means of Natural Selection, or the Preservation of Favoured Races in the Struggle for Life* in 1859 (Darwin, 1979 [1859]). One source of this stability of defense is that, in debates between creationist and evolutionists, creationists tend to deliver pre-set lectures (Shermer, 1997: 136) in which they repeat similar arguments though the emphasis changes over time.

The third chapter describes the general features of evolution in relation to statements made by scientific creationists. I point out some of the strengths of the evolutionary framework in response to criticisms of evolution by scientific creationists. I support in part Daniel C. Dennett's position in his work *Darwin's Dangerous Idea* (1995) that Darwin's ideas provide the best set of explanations for the diversity of life and humanity's place in the world today. There simply is no better framework explaining so much. Of course, scientific creationists argue their literal reading of the first eleven chapters of Genesis offers a better worldview. Thomas Kuhn (1970) has noted that a theory does not have to be perfect. It only has to have better explanatory powers than competing theories. Orthodox scientists are convinced that scientific creationism is greatly inferior to evolutionary models in explaining the biological variability on today's earth and in the past.

The fourth chapter presents the major features of scientific creationism and the scientific creationists' interpretation of the first eleven chapters of the Book of Genesis. Scientific creationism is currently the dominant and most effective voice among creationism. This group, along with intelligent design proponents, contains supporters who are both articulate and aggressively anti-evolution.

The fifth and sixth chapters deal with the central elements of scientific creationism. The Genesis flood and the year-long voyage of Noah's ark form the core of scientific creationist beliefs. These events have to be explained and defended before scientific creationism can achieve a reputation for scientific accuracy. The attempts to defend these beliefs result in complete disagreement with orthodox science, and so-called research based on the assumptions of the Noachian flood and the ark has not impressed orthodox scientists. The absurdities of trying to rationalize the events connected with the Genesis flood and Noah's ark force scientific creationists to spin improbable tissues of ad hoc hypotheses, "just-so" stories, and implausible rationalizations convincing only to their religious supporters.

The seventh chapter deals with the latest intellectual development of scientific creationism. Intelligent design has become a dominant approach in scientific creationism and is currently its most sophisticated version.

The last chapter deals with the current status of the creation/evolution controversy and its possible future. I predict that the creationist-evolution controversy will not go away but rather will increase in scope and intensity.

The Appendix lists some of the most important works currently dealing with creationism and evolution. While no short list can give justice to the large amount of effort scientific creationists and evolutionists have devoted to defending their separate cause and in attacking their opposites, the included works provide an understanding of the basic features and concerns of each side of the controversy.

Honesty forces me to be clear as to my perspective. I believe scientific creationism has no validity as a science. I present the arguments made by creationists to show their invalidity. Scientific creationists have presented their case in many venues and I show the arguments of scientific creationists are false, misleading, highly selective, or irrelevant.

Creationism

ooooooooooooooooooooooooooooooooooo

In the beginning God created the heaven and earth…So God created man in his own image, in the image of God created he him; male and female created he them.

—Genesis 1:1 and 1:27

Introduction

Creationism includes a variety of theologies. All have in common the belief a supernatural force has intervened in history to create life and to give it direction. Many creationists accept the Jewish and Christian Bibles as completely true in a literal manner and as a guide to secular knowledge. This characteristic of Biblical literalism places these creationists in the Protestant fundamentalist category. Fundamentalists have reverence for Biblical texts that preclude seeing scriptures as symbolic of deeper truths unless so indicated within the context of the passages. Scientific creationists also hold the Bible, if properly understood and interpreted, is a scientific as well as a religious document.

Reverence for scriptures in their literal state leads to a search in the scriptures for information and guidance (Crapanzano, 1999). What does not support Biblical passages should be rejected. John C. Whitcomb, a founder of the scientific creationist movement, states (Whitcomb, 1988: 123) "*The basic Christian presupposition of the inerrancy and perspicuity of the Genesis record must be maintained* (emphasis in the original)."

Several groups of creationists do not fit in the fundamentalist category. These more liberal creationists accept evolution within a Biblical framework. These creationists see the Jewish and Christian Bibles in a symbolic rather than in a literal manner.

Scientific creationists are fundamentalists who focus their attention on the book of Genesis. More liberal Christians are willing to accept the Bible as a gen-

11

eral guide that often must be interpreted and understood symbolically. Scientific creationists, by contrast, insist the Bible be understood in a literal fashion not only within the context of belief but also in all matters discussed in the Bible. Scientific creationists also believe the Bible is a reliable guide for the development of modern knowledge. Fundamentalist theologian Harold Lindsell (1976: 18) expresses the nature of Biblical literalism best:

> The bible is infallible or inerrant. It communicates religious truth, not religious error. But there is more. Whatever it communicates is to be trusted and can be relied upon as being true. The Bible is not a textbook on chemistry, astronomy, philosophy, or medicine. *But when it speaks on matters having to do with these or any other subjects*, the Bible does not lie to us. It does not contain error of any kind. Thus, the Bible, if true in all parts, cannot possibly teach that the earth is flat, that two and two make five, or that events happened at times other than we know they did (emphasis added).

Scientific creationist leader Henry M. Morris (1984: 20) holds a similar view representative of contemporary scientific creationists:

> The Bible authors claim to have written the very Word of God, and it has been accepted as such by multitudes of intelligent people down through the centuries. This is more true today than ever in the past, and there are now thousands of qualified scientists around the world who quite definitely believe in the full verbal inerrancy of the Holy Scriptures. It is thus absurd for anyone to say that "science" has disproved the Bible.
>
> Whenever a Biblical passage deals either with a broad scientific principle or with some particular item of scientific data, it will inevitably be found on careful study to be fully accurate in its scientific insights. Often it will be found even to have anticipated scientific discoveries.

Scientific creationists insist miracles, or divine interventions, take precedent over natural law. They also literally accept scriptural passages describing the total destruction during a worldwide flood of all land-based animals, including all humans except Noah and seven family members. This belief necessitates other beliefs counter to well-established evidence.

There exist major doctrinal differences among creationists focusing on the book of Genesis, especially the first eleven chapters. Creationists disagree among themselves in how long the six days of creation lasted and whether the ancestors of contemporary plants, animals, and humans were created at the same time. All creationists with the exception of the theistic evolutionists and perhaps the intelligent design advocates (they have avoided making detailed theological statements) believe a Christian God-produced flood took place, though there is disagreement whether this flood was local or worldwide. Below are the major divisions among creationists:

1. Young-Earth Creationism (YEC)

2. Old-Earth Creationism (OEC)

3. Gap Creationism

4. Scientific Creationism

5. Intelligent Design (ID)

6. Theistic Evolutionism

Accusing Evolution of Causing Social Problems

Members of the first five categories of the creationist divisions are united in their complete rejection of evolution. They define evolution as a major enemy although they may disagree among each other in terms of their interpretations of selected Biblical scriptures. In spite of major theological differences, creationists downplay their conflicts with one another while attempting to present a façade of unanimity to the public. Among themselves, creationists are willing to denounce one another in the same way they criticize evolutionary theory.

Creationists do not oppose modern, practical science. They respect and use science and contemporary technology unlike anti-modern religious groups as the Amish. Creationists are comfortable with the modern world and they do not reject modern plumbing because hydraulic science is not based on Biblical principles. Nevertheless, they attack evolution as a secular philosophy that rejects three of their most strongly-held beliefs: God created all life, almost certainly in six literal days; humans were created through supernatural intervention; and life does not change to adapt to new environmental conditions except in minor ways. They also reject those parts of science threatening their belief in an active creator who created humans in his image. To creationists, humans would be not be unique in the animal world, have souls, be God's favorite creations, or be moral beings if they had evolved from lower-order animals. In addition, creationists fear evolutionary thought undermines morality and religious institutions.

Creationists strongly oppose evolution's fundamental belief that humans, as well as animals, developed through natural processes independent of supernatural agencies. Equally disturbing is evolutionists' rejection of the fall of humans from a perfect, God-given state into one of sin. Creationists also are disturbed by the evolutionists' rejection of the belief that imperfections, such as evil and death, were caused by human sinful nature.

A common rationale for creationists' attacks on evolutionary theory and knowledge is that they blame evolutionary thought for most evils in contemporary society. This strategy is used to encourage people into rejecting evolution not on its own empirical merits but in order to protect the morality of their children and to usher a new age of social perfection. The rejection of evolution thus becomes a simple means of reform. The foreword of Henry M. Morris' work *The Long War Against God* (1989: 10) states:

> Many layers of error have been built on the faulty foundation of evolutionism. Humanism is the natural result. If God is not central in all our thinking then man must be. Atheism is humanism's twin brother, and consistent evolutionists cannot logically believe in the personal God of the Bible, the God who is the Creator of all life. Abortion, infanticide, and euthanasia are logical behaviors for those who have so easily disposed of the image of God in the eternal soul of man...
>
> The average person neither knows nor cares much about the error of evolution, and yet his or her life is constantly being influenced by it. Pornography, adultery, divorce, homosexuality, premarital sex, the destruction of the nuclear family—all are weeds that have grown from Satan's big lie about the universe. We are now on the verge of adopting full-fledged animalism in human practice—promiscuity, vandalism, hedonism, even incipient cannibalism. Even the Holocaust is "explained" by evolution. Hitler's extermination of the Jews grew out of his desire to speed up the evolutionary process.

The "big lie" in the above quote is the evolutionary mode of thinking, which fundamentalist creationists believe was presented to humans by Satan when the Tower of Babel was being built. The above statement accuses a secular belief for leading humans into what fundamentalists define as sinful behavior more indicative of changing modern societies, including divorce and the "destruction of the nuclear family." Morris also accuses evolutionary thought for deviancy that has not yet happened such as "incipient cannibalism." Morris is also adamant in insisting one cannot believe both in evolution and remain a good Christian and he at one stroke dismisses all creationists who are not Young-Earth scientific creationists. The above quote also indicates how serious Young-Earth scientific creationists such as Morris are in seeking to eliminate all mention of evolution in school programs. To these persons, evolution is a dangerous and threatening system of thought that must be eradicated for the good of society.

Ken Ham is less intellectually sophisticated than Morris but he also continuously attacks evolution as the source of many of today's problems. His series of books and videos as well as his many public lectures and debates make Ham an important promoter of the view that belief in evolution is not only false but also the cause of today's major social disorders. In Ham's book *The Lie: Evolution* (1987), evolution is responsible for racism, pornography, homosexuality, wide spread lawlessness, drug use, why religion is banned from public schools, male chauvinism, and additional social and moral ills. Ham is equally insistent on the evil influence of evolution in his book *Did Adam Have a Belly Button?* Ham states in question-and-answer form (Ham, 1999: 128):

> Q. Does evolution actually cause evils like abortion?
>
> A. No, but it's true that the increasing acceptance of abortion, homosexuality, and so on have gone hand in hand as evolution has increased in popularity. Of course, that doesn't mean that every evolutionist is an abortionist, or every abortionist is an evolutionist.

Ham implies in the above answer and in others in the same book that evolution weakens the moral order. Other creationists make more direct accusations that evolution has caused today's major social and moral problems. By the way, Ham's answer to his book's title is that Adam and Eve did not have belly buttons because Adam and Eve were created as adults and therefore would not have umbilical scars. Ham goes on to say that when challenged by their descendants to prove they were the first man and woman, they could "...show their bare tummies and say, "Look, no belly button (Ham, 1999: 185).""

The above quote shows the tendency of fundamentalists to rely on the Bible for statements based on literal readings of selected passages and the addition of what I call "just-so" stories that are extensions of Biblical scriptures. Creationists do much with little data, or with no data at all, as I show throughout this book. Ham is not only more circumspect than many other creationists but he also has a sense of humor, a characteristic often lacking among creationists. This seriousness on the part of creationists is understandable considering their feeling that their values are threatened by evolutionary ways of perceiving nature. An example of a more heavy-handed sense of humor among creationists is Henry M. Morris's designation of evolutionism as "evil-utionism."

Creationists have long linked evolution with Satan. Early Christian church theologian and second-century Bishop of Smyrnia Polycarp denounced Biblical non-literalists as "first-born of Satan (Lindsell, 1976: 47)." Clergy attacking evolutionary theory during Darwin's lifetime frequently did the same. Kent E. Hovind (n.d.) similarly denounced evolution during the 1990s by stating, "Evolutionary theory is one of the most greatest hindrances to scientific research that there is...It prevents people from seeing the obvious." Creationist lecturer Kent Hovind (Hovind, n.d.) in his video *Creation Seminar* lectures that the Devil told humans dinosaurs lived millions of year ago and "this Satanic message" is taught in public school beginning in the first grade. Hovind believes dinosaurs could not adapt to the post-flood world and gradually died out or were exterminated by human hunters. He believes that modern sightings of the Loch Ness Monster, the Yeti, Bigfoot, and other unusual creatures are indications that a few dinosaurs and other survivors remain alive in isolated places throughout the world.

Earlier linkage between evolution and Satanism is found in George McCready Price's reaction to what he felt was the dismal performance of creationists during the 1925 John Scopes "monkey trial" (see chapter two). Price's major work *Modern Flood Theory of Geology* (1935) forms the basis of contemporary scientific creationism, though few creationists today admit the fact. Price vented his anger at William Jennings Bryan (chief prosecutor for the creationist legal team) by stating in a letter to a friend that (quoted in Numbers, 1998: 83):

> The whole affair was undoubtedly planned long ahead by the devil; it [the prosecution] was bungled by Bryan in almost every possible way; and the general results were a triumph for the devil's cause such as the world has seldom seen before or since.

Price assumes the devil caused what he perceives to be the humiliation of the creationist argument. There is no awareness the creationist cause was weak to begin with or that the pro-evolution defense was better. It was only during the 1960s that creationists changed their strategies to make them more compelling to outsiders, including the courts. Nevertheless, contemporary scientific creationists continue to also see a conspiracy among evolutionists (probably enabled by Satan) to "force" evolution on students.

Price was one of the few creationists believing the "monkey trial" was a victory for evolutionists, but he is not alone then or now in castigating evolutionists for being Satan's naive pawns at best and allies of evil forces at worst. This demonization of their opponents is a tradition among creationists remaining strong today. A generation after Price's denunciation of the "devil's cause," Braswell Deen, chief justice of the Georgia Circuit Court of Appeals blamed the acceptance of evolution as the cause of social problems when he said in an alliterative fashion during 1981 (quoted in Eve and Harrold, 1991: 94):

> This monkey mythology of Darwin is the cause of permissiveness, promiscuity, pills, prophylactics, perversions, abortions, pornography, pollution, poisoning, and proliferation of crimes of all types.

John B. Thompson (1990: 65) describes this rhetorical strategy as the *expurgation of the other*, in which an opponent's theory is denounced as innately evil and false without directly challenging the rival's factual statements. The aim of this strategy is to scare listeners without attacking opponents' facts.

William Jennings Bryan, three-time presidential candidate, populist, and reformer, is one of the more famous creationists who felt evolutionary principles led to modern ills and disorder. Bryan prosecuted the anti-evolution case during the Scopes trial in 1925. His motivation to be the lead prosecutor in the "monkey trial" was influenced by his belief that the Darwinian principle of "survival of the fittest" encouraged global war and the decline he thought he observed in the morality of the American population. During the Scopes trial, Bryan linked Darwinism to Nietzsche, war, and atheism (De Camp, 1968: 330):

> I want to show that Nietzsche did praise Darwin. He put him as one of the three great men of his century. He put Napoleon first, because Napoleon had made war respectable. And he put Darwin among the three great men; his supermen were merely the logical outgrowth of the survival of the fittest with will and power; the only natural, logical outcome of evolution. And Nietzsche himself became an atheist following that doctrine, and became insane, and his father and mother and uncle were among the people he tried to kill.

More recently, an account of a former Italian fascist, now a Christian missionary, linked fascism to evolutionary theory (Wieland, 2003: 32):

> Among the bitterest enemies of fascism were the communists. This was ironic, since their equally totalitarian, ruthless philosophy also owed a great deal to the surge of materialism/atheism resulting from Darwin's teachings.

There are no attempts to prove such charges other than to declare the danger of evolutionary thought. Scientific creationists make the serious error of believing a scientific discipline that does not include a theistic element must by definition be atheistic and anti-creationist. They ignore the fact that science is neutral in terms of the supernatural. A physician who ignores the possibility that an illness such as AIDS is the result of sinful behavior is not necessarily an atheist.

Internal Dissention Among Creationists

Creationists downplay differences among themselves. Their view is that unity is necessary at this time in order to defeat the greater enemy: evolutionary theory. Theological disagreements can be resolved after evolutionary theory is no longer dominant in the schools. In spite of this temporary tolerance, reactionary scientific creationists such as Morris and Ham believe any weakening of a literal interpretation of Genesis is mistaken and almost as dangerous as atheism. Nevertheless, creationists expend their energy attacking evolution rather than other fundamentalists holding a different interpretation of Genesis. Joyce L. Gibson (1999: *xx* and 7) is typical of those who wish to avoid any public theological controversy:

> One date people are especially interested in is the date when the universe began. You will not find that date in Genesis—not even a hint! What you will find is where the universe came from and who created life and made the first man and woman.
>
> Just how old is the world? Are we living on an Old Earth or a Young Earth? No matter how we answer the question, we have to base our answer on incomplete information in the Bible. God has chosen not to give us the date.

Gibson, however, is in the minority. Scientific creationists expect detailed and definite answers from their scriptures and they are willing to add their own guesses when the scriptures are vague or incomplete. While scientific creationists such as Henry M. Morris insist that the Bible offers complete information, Gibson represents a rare neutral position among creationists. The more radical among their ranks are currently the most vocal, the best organized and funded, and the most prolific in producing books, articles, and even comic books to present their views. These creationists wish to have their particular brand of creationism taught in school science curricula. Public theological disagreements would begin after creationism is taught in public schools. At that time, school programs would contain multiple theological debates based on differing interpretations of scripture.

Among themselves, creationists criticize one another while publications meant for the general public seldom contain material critical of other creationists. Henry

M. Morris criticized theistic evolutionists in the periodical *Bibliotheca Sacra* in the strongest terms by quoting Biblical verses (Romans 1:22, 23, 25, 28) denouncing those who "...changed the truth of God into a lie, and worshipped and served the creature more than the Creator..." Morris concluded by linking evolution to Satan (Morris, 1966: 148–9):

> They [theistic evolutionists] do not like to retain God in their knowledge, and they abhor the thought of His coming one day to judge them. And if God is going to be ignored or rejected, then the only possible way in which the existence of the universe and its inhabitants can be explained is in terms of evolution. Evolution is an absolute necessity for anyone who would dethrone God. In the last analysis, therefore, the evolutionary philosophy must have its origin and rationale in the rebellion of Satan himself, who is engaged in an agelong war against God, seeking to usurp His place as King of the universe...A man cannot be *truly* Christian or altruistic, or even scientific, and also believe in evolution.

Almost all Christians were Young-Earth creationists in one form or another until the end of the eighteenth century. By the early 1800s, the newly developed science of geology convinced many thoughtful persons the earth was not created roughly six thousand years ago, as Irish Archbishop James Ussher computed in 1654. A contemporary of Ussher, John Lightfoot, refined Ussher's computations with his declaration that Adam was created at nine a.m. on October 4, 4004 B.C. Conservative Christians accepted the date of 4004 B.C. for the creation of the universe. Although there have been other attempts to determine the exact or near-exact date of creation, fundamentalist scientific creationists are satisfied with the estimate that the six-day creation occurred roughly six to eleven thousand years ago.

A curious example of the doubts intellectuals held concerning the Biblical creation myth during the 1700s and 1800s was the evolutionary beliefs of Charles Darwin's grandfather, Erasmus Darwin (1731–1803). Erasmus Darwin published *Zoönomia* during the last decade of the eighteenth century. It is an epic in verse discussing evolution and other unorthodox topics of the day. Erasmus Darwin stated in *Zoönomia: Or, The Laws of Organic Life* that animals adapted to changing environments and could express strong emotions. The work was so radical that the Roman Catholic Church placed it on its index of banned books. Erasmus Darwin was unusual for his time because he also believed all organisms descended from a simple organism (Irvine, 1955: 85), which in turn emerged out of primordial seas millions of years ago (Birx, 1991: 53).

Although Charles Darwin read his grandfather's work with interest and developed similar ideas, he was not impressed because *Zoönomia* is based on personal insights rather than facts. Darwin believed observation and theory went together and he distrusted any work based only on speculation.

By the early 1800s, most educated persons in England and the United States were evolutionists in one sense or another and creationists as well. Darwinism, often in modified form, began to be accepted by the majority of intellectuals during the second half of the nineteenth century. Most scientists in the United States became evolutionists, as were most university professors. Most theological and seminary faculty accepted evolutionary principles, though some hid their acceptance of evolution. After the First World War, when more fundamentalists enrolled in state universities and religious colleges, fundamentalists found higher education was dominated by liberal theologians or by completely secular professors. Those who insisted on strict Biblical literalism found themselves an embarrassed minority in most theological schools.

Fundamentalists increasingly focused their efforts on reforming targets they could influence. They soon realized that the ideas of evolution and an old earth were too entrenched at the university level. The battle for ideology turned to public education at the high school level when students are first introduced to the biological sciences and evolution. Creationists also began to use their political influence to attempt to drive evolution out of public school curricula. By the early 1920s, a number of local school boards and state legislatures had passed anti-evolution laws. The struggle had begun to determine whether evolution or creationism would prevail in the classroom.

Young-Earth Creationism

Young-Earth creationists are the dominant voices in the current creation/evolution controversy. There are two main branches of Young-Earth creationists. One branch developed into the scientific creationists (see below). The other Young-Earth creationists are the more traditional and are less interested in combining science and scriptures to defend their beliefs. Contemporary scientific creationists believe the Bible is as reliable as science when scripture discusses an issue. They also believe science, if properly understood, supports Biblical scripture. This position necessitates a literal interpretation of the book of Genesis of the Jewish Bible. Henry M. Morris and John C. Whitcomb are among the most influential authors of the Young-Earth scientific creationists. Morris is an extremely prolific writer and his works form the foundation of contemporary beliefs about Young-Earth creationism. Henry M. Morris and his son, John D. Morris, believe Genesis provides exact and correct descriptions of the creation of the universe and life (Morris and Morris, 1996: 13–4):

> Rather than outmoded folklore, as most critics allege, the creation chapters of Genesis are marvelous and accurate accounts of the *actual events* of the primeval history of the universe.

Young-Earth creationists accept five propositions that form the basis of most defenses of the contemporary scientific creationist position (adapted from Gough, 1983: 26):

- The universe and all matter were created roughly six to ten thousand years ago.

- A supernatural agent created life suddenly roughly six to ten thousand years ago.

- A worldwide flood occurred four thousand years ago.

- The Bible must be understood in its literal sense unless the context indicates a passage is to be taken symbolically.

- All animals have fixed genetic make ups that allow only minor changes (microevolution) over time. Natural processes cannot create new species.

Young-Earth creationists (YECs) face great challenges when defending their position. They disagree with orthodox geologists who deny the earth is more than six thousand years old. Young-Earth creationists are forced to ignore vast amounts of geological evidence. They defend themselves in large part by proposing ad hoc hypotheses ("just-so" stories) contradicting established facts. Many of these positions are presented and criticized in later chapters. A typical conflict between Young-Earth creationists and orthodox scientists deals with the evidence of previous numerous ice ages. It is clear from the evidence that many ice ages occurred over a span of millions of years. Young-Earth creationists hold there was only one ice age shortly after the flood and that the polar caps developed roughly four thousand years ago. There was more water on the earth's surface immediately after the flood and the temperature of this water was high enough to cause precipitation for perhaps hundreds of years that later created the polar ice caps. Such statements lie outside established scientific knowledge and are defended by untestable claims.

Young-Earth creationists do not like the term "Young-Earth" since they feel the earth is as old as it is and the term suggests some type of comparison. They are, however, stuck with the term. In addition to quarrels with orthodox geologists, Young-Earth creationists insist all organisms were created fully developed during one brief period. The process of how this was done is unknown but the emergence of new types of animals is impossible. YECs also believe life could never come into being through natural laws alone and therefore a creator is necessary (Nelson and Reynolds, 1999: 44) to explain life's presence and diversity.

YECs insist belief in evolution leads to a rejection of original sin, the need to be saved, and the belief God established moral rules of behavior. They reject evolution in large part because they feel a belief in evolution causes people to reject religious principles. Evolution and evolutionists are therefore seen as immoral opponents of a well-defined religious morality.

One minor variant of the Young-Earth ideology is the mature-earth model. Mature-earth proponents accept the Young-Earth proposition, but add God created the earth and universe to *appear* to be of great age. Just as God created Adam and Eve as adults, God created suns of different ages and light beams that seem as if they have been traveling for billions of years and an earth that seems to be billions of years old (Wise, 2002: 66). This perspective avoids denying the validity of dating methodologies showing the earth and organic remains to be older than ten thousand years. Unfortunately, this view accepts the notion God is a trickster who lies. Such a view makes a mockery of scientific regularities since any discrepancy in nature can be explained away by saying God is lying or created false evidence.

Old-Earth Creationism

Old-Earth creationists (OECs) accept geological time. OECs interpret the term "day" in Genesis as an indefinite period lasting for thousands, millions, or even billions of years. OECs have accommodated their beliefs to geological ("deep") time and the evidence from fossils that life is more than six thousand years old. Well-respected OEC Walter L. Bradley, who falls in the Old-Earth/intelligent design creationist categories, feels a forty-day flood cannot explain the geological evidence of fossils and multiple layers of soil. He notes the Gulf of Mexico contains fossils in sedimentary layers that are as much as 25,000 feet deep. Each layer of sediment was deposited under different conditions and contains different types of fossils (see Moreland and Reynolds, 1999: 77). Bradley is typical of those since the early 1800s who recognize the overwhelming evidence for geological time.

Bradley is also representative of creationists who interpret the passage that Adam and Eve would "surely die" in Genesis 2:17 as a consequence disobeying God's commandment to refrain from eating the fruit on the tree of life as a spiritual death rather than a physical death. This interpretation of a central scripture allows OECs to accept the evidence that living creatures lived *and died* before the fall of Adam and Eve. By contrast, Young-Earth creationists cannot accept the belief that organisms died before the fall because they interpret Genesis 2:17 to mean the fall caused death to appear for the first time. YECs believe there was no death before the expulsion from Eden and that Adam and Eve, their children, and all organisms then present would have lived forever. In addition, YECs hold that, until the flood, all animals lived in harmony with humanity. Animals and humans were vegetarian before the flood and therefore did not fear each other.

William Jennings Bryan testified during the Scopes trial he was an Old-Earth creationist (Numbers, 1998: 80) though he also admitted he did not believe there was any significance in whether God's creative period was six days or six millennia. This issue was not an important one for many fundamentalists at that time though it now reflects a major division among fundamentalists.

The Jehovah's Witnesses is an example of anti-evolution Old-Earth creationism. Founded during the 1880s as a reaction against liberal trends such as Biblical criticism and acceptance of evolution, the group now numbers almost six million members worldwide and almost a million in the United States. Witnesses are Biblical literalists and have been forced to publish their own edition of the Bible in order to change what they consider are translation errors in earlier editions. Witnesses believe the six days of creation were each longer than twenty-four hours. This allows them to accept geologic time spanning possibly billions of years with the assumption the present "day" is already thousands of years old. They nevertheless totally reject evolution. Witnesses' anti-evolution rhetoric includes the standard arguments made by Young-Earth creationist groups. They also accept microevolution but not macroevolution (Watch Tower & Bible Tract Society of Pennsylvania, 1967: 55–6):

> Various species of plants and animals have adapted to different circumstances, such as climatic changes. Is this evidence of evolution? No, because plants and animals are not first non-adapted and then become adapted. They already have within their organisms the possibility of lesser or greater adaptation. The cactus did not evolve into a cactus from a different plant just because the climate became dry. *Some features may become accentuated in severe climatic changes, but that possibility of variation was there to begin with* (emphasis added).

Jehovah's Witnesses accept the intelligent design argument that life is too complex to have evolved (see below). They also reject the notion God created imperfect organisms needing to evolve. Witnesses also depend heavily on the argument that evolutionists disagree among themselves thereby showing evolution must be false. Another rhetorical strategy is the suggestion evolution is not a reasonable alternative to creationism (Watch Tower & Bible Tract Society of Pennsylvania, 1998: 14–5):

> Can experts now explain the origin of the universe? Many scientists, uncomfortable with the idea that the universe was created by a higher intelligence, speculate that by some mechanism it created itself out of nothing. Does that sound reasonable to you?

The strategy of ridiculing evolution as "unreasonable" allows Witnesses to reject any evidence supporting evolution as unreasonable without having to disprove its validity.

Gap Creationism

Gap creationism (sometimes characterized as "ruin and restoration") was first proposed during the early 1830s when geological discoveries made Young-Earth creationism harder to accept. Gap creationism was common dogma until the emergence in the early 1960s of the now dominant Young-Earth scientific creationism. An acceptance of a gap of time allows fundamentalists to both denounce evolution and accept the overwhelming evidence for an old earth. Gap creationists also do not have to explain fossil placement as the result of a yearlong flood. They do not have to explain how plants were created on the third day of creation while the sun was created during the fourth "day."

Gap creationism developed from a specific reading of the second verse of Genesis 1:

> And the earth *was* without form, and void; and darkness was upon the face of the deep. And the Spirit of god moved on the face of the waters [emphasis added].

Gap creationists translate the first "was" in the above verse as "became." This allows the verse ("…and the earth became without form…") to describe a creation that became "without form [i.e., destroyed]" to be re-created as described in Genesis. Theologians could now infer from this passage a time period between creation and the cataclysm, thus allowing for geological time. Since the earth was now "without form and void," one could believe God re-created order and life in the six-day creation period described in Genesis. Fossils come from the earlier stage of creation.

The origin of life according to gap creationists may have been due to the fall of Lucifer and his transformation from an angel to the evil Satan. Some gap creationists assume God re-created life to show Satan His power after Satan and his cohort revolted (Pennock, 1999: 77). The universe as a whole was not destroyed presumably because God either did not need to show His power to that extent or because the behavior making destruction necessary occurred only on the earth. The time between the first creation and the second six-day period is indeterminate but assumed to be extremely long. Young-Earth creationists reject gap creationism and feel an acceptance of gapism leads not only to heresy but to possible acceptance of evolution (McIver, 1988: 4).

Georges Cuvier (1769–1832), founder of the science of paleontology, tried to accommodate then-current creationist beliefs with the large numbers of fossils excavated during the early nineteenth century in France and elsewhere. He noted the large number of extinct organisms at different geological levels suggested a time span of more than the Biblical six thousand years. Cuvier, the leader in comparative anatomy, decided the fossil evidence showed the earth had experienced a series of floods and major catastrophes during which most animals were destroyed during separate eras. God created more, often very different, animals after each catastrophe. Most scientists during the first part of the nineteenth century accepted Cuvier's views because his theory seemed to explain the layers of fossils being discovered throughout the world.

Cuvier compared the anatomies of modern storks with mummified Egyptian storks and found no changes in bone structure had taken place. This finding suggested to Cuvier that the earth was very old and changes among animals took place very slowly, if at all, until a catastrophe occurred. It was obvious from observation that fossils, which are very different in physical structure from living organisms, must have lived more than six to ten thousand years ago and therefore are older than a literal reading of the Bible would suggest.

Gap creationism was the dominant view among creationists until the 1960s, when Young-Earth scientific creationists began to take center stage and dominate the creation-evolution debate. The authoritative 1909 edition of the *Scofield Reference Bible* included the acceptance of two creations, with a gap of an indefinite amount of time derived from Cyrus I. Scofield's interpretation of Genesis 1:1. Gap creationists easily accommodate themselves to the existence of fossils and the evidence of long-term geologic time by the acceptance of two separate creation periods. The first creation period took place "in the beginning" when "one year is with the Lord as a thousand years (2Peter 3:8)." The first period lasted eons. Some gap creationists believed the earth was being "prepared" for humans during that time.

The second period of creation began roughly six thousand years ago (around 4,004 B.C.). The period between the creation of the universe and the creation of Adam and Eve is called the "gap." The gap can be understood as God's special creation. In addition, gap proponents believe that God set processes in motion that needed time to develop fully.

The gap theory is based on a unique interpretation of verses 1:1 and 1:2 of the Book of Genesis. Part of the disagreement between gap creationists and other creationists lies in the interpretation of the Hebrew word *waw* at the start of the second verse. *Waw* can be translated as "and" or "but." Gap creationists use the "but" translation (Morris, 1985: 232) which suggests a destruction of the first creation.

Charles Darwin and others, notably Charles Lyell (1797–1875), discredited the gap theory that the pre-Adamic earth experienced a series of complete catastrophes. Lyell's influential three volume *Principles of Geology* (1830–3) established the science of geology based on uniformitarianism. The uniformitarian view proposes the earth's features were formed through natural causes such as erosion and the sinking/rising of the continents over a long period of time. Lyell insisted geological changes occurred through natural laws without divine intervention rather than as the result of a God-produced series of catastrophes. Lyell's work influenced Darwin's thinking and Darwin's theory of natural selection revolutionized biology in the same way Lyell's work revolutionized geology. Both saw change in their respective fields as taking place in slow steps over a great length of time through the operation of natural rather than supernatural causes.

Modern scientific creationists reject the gap theory on both scriptural and geological grounds (Morris, 1985: 42). Scientific creationists reject the gap theory because it allows for an interpretation of the length of days during the six days of creation and thereby violates the principle of Biblical literalism. Scientific creationists also insist all geological formations were produced during the Genesis flood or soon after. By contrast, gap creationists accept geological formations indicating the earth's great age. Scientific creationists also totally reject the gap creationists' statement that animals died before Adam and Eve were expulsed from the Garden of Eden. As Henry M. Morris (1976: 47) states:

Fossils, however, are dead things! They speak clearly of a work in which suffering, disease, and death—often violent, widespread death—were universal realities...If that world existed prior to the supposed pre-Adamic cataclysm, then it existed before the sin of Satan which brought on the cataclysm. That is, suffering and death existed for a billion years before the sin of Satan and the subsequent sin of Adam.

This point is significant for modern Young-Earth creationists because they hold strongly the belief a perfect world without death once existed. The expulsion from the Garden of Eden and the introduction of death remind Young-Earth creationists there is a penalty for sin and violation of God's commandments.

Scientific Creationism

Scientific creationists maintain life began roughly six to ten thousand years ago and animals and plant fossils were formed around 3000 B.C. during a worldwide flood. They reject the notion humans descended from ape-like ancestors. Their Biblical readings tell them the nature and physiology of humans and all other living organisms are stable except for instances of microevolution, such as the differences from one breed of dog to another. Genetic change can only take place within species, making the development of new species impossible.

Scientific creationists accept the axiom that science is based on fact and proof. They differ with evolutionists in that scientific creationists do not believe evolution has been demonstrated to be true. As important, however, scientific creationists also believe the Bible is as accurate as scientific statements. In fact, the Bible is deemed to be correct when there is a conflict between established scientific knowledge and scripture. The scriptures are superior to contemporary science and any conflict between the two is a reflection of error on the part of secular science.

Scientific creationists respect science and wrap themselves in the mantle of orthodox science without success. Scientific creationists such as Henry M. Morris have published books on creationist topics without reference to scripture by using pseudo-scientific statements to "prove" evolution is incorrect and the Bible can be the basis for empirical studies, such as proving a global flood occurred or that fossils are less than ten thousand years old. Creationists believe themselves to be scientists taking into account Biblical scripture (Marsden, 1980: 214).

Scientific creationists are also hostile toward theistic evolutionists. Henry M. Morris accuses Christian evolutionists of being potential atheists and he rejects any connection with anyone who does not accept a literal six-day creation period.

Morris stated his position in his usually clear prose in the following editorial in his organization's monthly newsletter *Acts & Facts* (quoted in Schaderwald, 1983: 48–9):

> But can't we be *Christian* evolutionists, they say? Yes, no doubt it is possible to be a Christian evolutionist. Likewise, one can be a Christian thief, or a Christian adulterer, or a Christian liar! Christians can be inconsistent and illogical about many things, but that doesn't make them right.

Scientific creationists use the ideas of Thomas S. Kuhn (1970) to buttress their claim that scientific creationism is as scientific as orthodox science. Kuhn notes there is a central body of knowledge that dominates thought and becomes the official statement on a set of phenomena and becomes established as orthodox or normal science. Leading practitioners dominate the journals, conferences, and grant-awarding institutions. Those who disagree find that they have little audience for their ideas and are either ridiculed or ignored. Orthodox, official science is based on a major paradigm being given respect while all other models are rejected. Scientific creationists believe evolutionists wrongly ignore their own paradigm.

This characterization of Kuhn's work is correct as presented by creationists, but this is only part of Kuhn's contribution to the nature of science. Scientific creationists ignore the fact is science is self-correcting. Models lacking conviction are refined until they better fit observations and experimental data or are rejected. Scientists are expected to be tolerant of competing models but they are not expected to accept a model after it has been proven to be inadequate (Kitcher, 1982: 168).

Orthodox scholars find scientific creationism too based on religious values and scriptures to offer reliable empirical knowledge. Further, too much evidence exists contradicting all of scientific creationists' statements. Many of the creationists' statements were rejected by start of the nineteenth century and Charles Darwin was only one of many who showed through their empirical analyses the Young-Earth creationist view conflicted with the growing evidence the earth was more than ten thousand years old.

Scientific creationists believe their Young-Earth creationist paradigm is correct and is unfairly rejected by influential orthodox scientists. They believe they have proven evolution is incorrect and only stubborn blindness keeps their creationist paradigm from being accepted. In addition, scientific creationists believe that many facts can be interpreted differently whether one uses the Bible or natural laws as a guide. This belief allows scientific creationists to demand that schools include both evolution and creationism in their science material on the basis both are equally valid in terms of how phenomena can be interpreted. At the very least, scientific creationists demand teachers be allowed the freedom to point out to students the weaknesses of the evolutionary model as shown by scientific creationism.

On their part, scientists following a non-Biblical naturalist model believe scientific creationism ignores too many facts to be either valid or an acceptable science. Naturalistic scientists also feel that the Biblical basis of scientific creationism precludes it from being considered as an orthodox science. Normal scientists also feel scientific creationism is not scientific because scientific creationists do not test their assumptions and therefore should be considered as religious ideology and religious apologetics rather than as true science. Scientists do not accept the scientific creationist claim that the creationist position is as scientific as evolutionary theory and as a result they reject the proposition scientific creationism should be given equal time in science curricula in public schools.

Scientific creationists insist on dismissing evolution because not everything is known about the process and mechanisms of evolution. They insist that evolution can be discredited if they can point to the limitations of evolutionary thought and knowledge. As a result, scientific creationists are quick to point out whenever evolutionists disagree with one another. They fail to note that evolutionists disagree among each other because there are a number of Kuhn-like competing models within evolution. The fact evolutionists disagree merely means the discipline is an on-going affair and subject to both knowledge accumulation and change of emphasis. From Kuhn, we accept the fact that scientists will disagree with one another, and that this competition is one of the most powerful mechanisms for the development of scientific knowledge. There is a "survival of the fittest" struggle in science as well as in nature.

Although scientific creationists claim to be as scientific as orthodox scientists, the basis of scientific creationism is Biblical rather than empirical. The fact that scientific creationists reject any attempts to change their religious views when faced with contrary evidence suggests their position is religious rather than scientific.

Intelligent Design

Intelligent design (ID) offers the greatest challenge currently faced by contemporary evolutionists wishing to keep creationist material out of public school curricula. ID proponents present the argument that complexity in organisms and in the universe cannot be explained by current evolutionary knowledge. Complexity in nature, such as an eye or a multi-step biological process, suggests design. Design in turn reflects the handiwork of a designer, by implication the Christian God. Charles Darwin took the notion of a supernatural designer out of biology and replaced it with the concept of natural selection. Darwin presented natural selection as the alternative to theistic design and it remains the major alternative to the religious argument for design.

ID defenders insist they can re-introduce proof of design back into biology. Proponents of the intelligent design argument assume that there is a limit to what evolution can explain, if anything. Their core belief is that life is too complicated to have developed in a random, non-directed fashion. Design (complexity) proves the existence of a God and the existence of a purposeful and meaningful universe since many biological processes have too low probabilities to have emerged through evolutionary means and natural.

Intelligent design is a new form of the attacks on evolution scientific creationists have been making since at least the 1960s. The agenda is still the same: to discredit evolution so religious beliefs can be taught in schools. The specific danger of introducing the intelligent design approach in science curricula is that it would encourage students to accept the view some topics cannot be studied because their complexity indicates supernatural intervention.

In addition, intelligent design creationists are led by the Jewish and Christian Bibles rather than by empirical speculations. Designer scientist Leonard Brand admits that Biblical sources form the foundations for the intelligent design orientation, though he does not show why his religious beliefs are more useful in explaining nature than the scriptures of other religions (Brand, 1997: 318):

> To me, the exciting thing is that, when we allow the Scriptures to aid us in developing hypothese about earth history, we can successsfully use these hypotheses to guide us in productive research.

Brand prefers the term "informed interventionist" rather than "creationist." He nevertheless believes the Bible as well as nature offers clues to the existence of a designer.

Theistic Evolutionism

Theistic evolutionists are Old-Earth creationists who believe God used natural processes such as evolution to achieve the contemporary features of the earth, life and humanity. Some believe God guides evolution at specific times so evolution eventually achieves the proper goals established by God. In this context, evolution has a purpose and the universe has a moral dimension. Theistic evolution re-inserts the elements of the supernatural and moral meaning into the universe (Miller, 1999). Scientific creationists and Young-Earth creationists reject theistic evolutionism as a rejection of a literal understanding of the scriptures and as a compromise ultimately leading to atheism. Berghoef and Dekoster (1989) place theistic evolution and materialistic evolution in the same atheistic category. Henry M. Morris (1977: 12) similarly views theistic evolution as faith gone wrong. Morris (1985: 93–4) denounces Christians who do not accept the literal meaning of the Bible in this way:

> Creationists, however, have long maintained that theistic evolution is actually a contradiction in terms, like "Christian atheism." If evolution is able to explain all forms of life, as leading evolutionists insist, then God is redundant. Furthermore, the very essence of evolution is one of chance variations, waste, inefficiency, struggle and survival or extinction. The very terms are inconsistent with a God of wisdom and power, and with the ethics of Christianity.

Theistic evolutionists also reject the philosophical position that the universe is a mechanical object with no purpose, meaning, or direction. Instead, they insist evolution is part of a meaningful unfolding purpose. The universe has a history pointing to a specific goal since fossil evidence indicates a progression from simple to complex and from instinct to consciousness. This, of course, is a very attractive view of the universe because it gives meaning to life. The alternative is a view of evolution without external purpose, meaning, or direction. Richard Dawkins, Daniel Dennett, and Stephen Jay Gould are examples of evolutionists who deny any purpose or direction in evolution.

Theistic evolutionists accept the notion of a creator who allows natural laws to direct evolution, though some feel that God intervenes at critical times. Other theistic evolutionists prefer to define God as a watchmaker who created life but allows evolution to develop along predetermined paths without needing any additional supernatural guidance. Although theistic evolutionists disagree among themselves in terms of their philosophical and theological frameworks, all agree the universe has meaning and direction toward greater union with God. All theistic evolutionists include the notion of change as a core element. They view God as a source of change while God Himself changes and nature, humanity, and God are all developing (Barbour, 1997: 104–5). God uses evolution to allow humanity the freedom and spontaneity to freely realize God's love. Theistic evolution brings back to the cosmos a purpose and direction orthodox scientists have more or less rejected.

Theistic evolutionists believe evolution increases man's realization of God. They reject the notion that nature is without fault, contrary to the scientific creationists. These process philosophers also stress the universe and God are in constant flux and change (i.e. development) is inherent in life. Alfred N. Whitehead, Charles Pierce, and Charles Hartshorne are among the leading advocates for the existence of an evolutionary process as a central characteristic of both the universe and God (Hartshorne 1970: 160):

> [God] is an individual, eminently acting upon and eminently receiving influences from the nondivine individuals. The "glory of God" is neither God apart from the world, nor the world and God, but the world taken into the divine life.

The largest Christian theistic evolutionist group is the Roman Catholic Church. On October 22, 1996, Pope John Paul II re-affirmed the church's position on evolution in his statement "Truth Cannot Contradict Truth." The members of the Pontifical Academy of Sciences had recently investigated the Church's relationships to science during the 16th through the 18th centuries. This program was part of the general theme "reflection on science at the dawn of the third millennium." The general conclusion of the members of the Academy was that science and religion were not in opposition.

Pope Pius XII had earlier announced in 1950 there was no conflict between Church doctrine and evolution, even though he felt evolution had not been completely proven. Pope John Paul II implicitly re-affirmed this position in 1992 when the Church exonerated Galileo for his heretical statements about celestial mechanics. He stated that "new knowledge has led to the recognition of the theory of evolution as more than a hypothesis" though he rejected a completely material definition of the nature of humans (http://www.newadvent.org/docs/jp02tc.htm).

Pope John Paul II in 1996 stated Church theology insisted God was the creator, but that evolution could be accepted as a God-directed process. In this case, the Pope accepted the *fact* of evolution while the *mechanism* of evolution is defined as partly supernatural. Within this model, there exists a distinct difference between humans and other beings because only humans can:

> enter into a relationship of knowledge and love with God himself, a relationship which will find its complete fulfillment beyond *time*, in *eternity*. All the depth and grandeur of this vocation are revealed to us in the mystery of the *risen Christ*...It is by virtue of his *spiritual soul* that the whole person possesses such a dignity even in his body...if the human body take its origin from preexistent living matter, the spiritual soul is immediately created by God...

Roman Catholic doctrine insists on a spiritual dimension of humans, or a soul, enabling them to have a spiritual life and a moral conscience. Roman Catholic theology accepts evolution as a process but adds that the creator placed souls in humans at one point thereby making them morally and spiritually different from other organisms. A significant aspect of Pope John Paul II's 1996 announcement was his statement there was evidence for evolution and that evolutionary theory could not be contradicted by theology (Gould, 1997). He had accepted both the material nature of evolution as well as the spirituality of humanity.

One of the more influential and radical theistic evolutionists was Roman Catholic Marie-Joseph-Pierre Teilhard de Chardin (1881–1955). Officials of the Roman Catholic Church silenced Teilhard's mystical views but his writings enjoyed cult popularity after his death. He joined the Society of Jesus in 1902, studied in a Jesuit institution in England, and taught in Cairo, Egypt. Teilhard became a respected archaeologist after the First World War and was sent to China in 1923 to excavate sites, including the location where the Peking Man was discovered. It was at this time that he wrote his first work, *The Divine Milieu* (1926), which included speculations on the place humans had in a God-directed evolution (Fry and Fry, 1989: 5). Teilhard proposed the "law of increasing complexity" or the process from the simple to the sophisticated contemporary evolutionists such as Stephen Jay Gould rejected as too mystical. The process of increasing complexity of organisms was for Teilhard evidence that God had a purpose for life within a natural framework. Teilhard's vision—he brings mysticism into science—is similar to the way scientific creationists bring their religious beliefs onto a scientific context. In Teilhard's case, fossil evidence suggested the existence of a force pushing humans toward a union with a personal God (Birx, 1991: 191) using the natural processes of evolution. This ever-closer awareness of God demands ever-higher levels of consciousness made possible by a developing nervous system (cerebralization) and brain, primarily the frontal lobes (cephaliza-tion).

Teilhard also proposed the complimentary principle of increasing conscious-ness. The increased size of the human brain and increasing complexity of nervous systems in organisms allow for a greater appreciation of God's cosmic love and glory. The purposes of evolution are the achievement of awareness of Alpha and Omega, or Christ and union with God. The end result of evolution is a collective spiritual union of all life making possible a God-humanity assimilation surround-ing the earth above the atmosphere (Birx, 1991: 98). Teilhard calls this envelope of consciousness the "theosphere." Teilhard is thoroughly part of the tradition giving a theological purpose and direction to evolutionary processes.

Summary

Creationism has many forms because creationists disagree among themselves. All creationists, however, believe a supernatural agency intervened in history to cre-ate the universe and life. The major voice today among creationists is the scien-tific creationist approach. Scientific creationism is also the most problematic form of creationism because scientific creationists demand the introduction of their religious views into science programs in public schools. This possible intermin-gling of science, education, and religion offers great harm to both the educational and scientific endeavors.

The next chapter deals with the most spectacular confrontations between evo-lutions and creationists. Each confrontation forced participants to present their best arguments. Each confrontation also illustrates the nature of creationist beliefs and their religious foundations.

Evolution on Trial

o o o o o o o o o o o o o o o o o o o o o o o o o o o o o o o o o o
One of the more disappointing aspects of the Scopes trial was its
intimidating effect on Christians.

—*Henry M. Morris*

Intellectuals, religious leaders, and educated persons in general reacted, at times
violently and emotionally, to Darwinism in its various forms. Fundamental Protestants, with their literal interpretations of Biblical scriptures, uniformly rejected
Darwinism and correctly identified this view of nature as a major challenge to
their own views. Although the majority of evolutionists in Europe and in the
United States also believed in God, acceptance of Darwinism demanded adjust-
ments of traditional theological beliefs, especially the literal interpretation of
Genesis. At first the controversy was limited to academic circles and among intellectuals already predisposed to accept some form of evolutionary theory. However, knowledge of the principles of Darwinism soon spread to the general public
and more conservative religious and scientific leaders. In England, the debate
between evolutionists and anti-evolutionists took place in universities, books,
periodicals, and newspapers.

By contrast, the general public in the United States often became aware of the
presence of Darwinist thought during church sermons and when creationists
sought to exclude Darwinism from public school biology curricula. Public
debates in the form of legal challenges became the flashpoints of the Darwinism-
creationism conflicts. The following sections describe the most significant examples of the confrontations between Darwinists and Protestant fundamentalists.

The Huxley-Wilberforce Debate

The first dramatic confrontation between creationists and evolutionists took
place just one year after Charles Darwin published his controversial book *The*

Origin of Species by Means of Natural Selection in 1859. Each faction controlled or influenced magazines and newspapers that published essays and book reviews supporting one side or the other. Many persons had already read or heard of Darwin's book and it became both a controversial work and a best seller.

The stage was set for a very public confrontation during the 1860 annual meetings of the British Association for the Advancement of Science at Oxford, England. The association met annually for a week with lectures, speeches, debates, and scientific presentations by notable scientists and concerned individuals, including clergy with scientific or natural history interests. Professional and amateur scientists delivered their latest findings, presented often in a very technical manner.

The general public as well as members also attended the association's sessions. It was fashionable during this era for interested persons to attend during the social season lectures by famous personages. Popular lecturers included Thomas Henry Huxley (1825–95), who had already become Darwin's most vocal and effective supporter. Popular lecturers were as sought after as today's movie and rock stars. In addition, there were few professional scientists supporting themselves through their work and a source of supplementary income for a dynamic speaker was the ability to attract large audiences and readers. Huxley was one of the first who had no other sources of financial support other than his lectureships, writings, and government subsidies and commissions.

By contrast, Darwin was typical of an older generation of amateurs who indulged their scientific interests as lifelong hobbies made possible by their inherited wealth. Darwin himself never worked for pay and supported himself through his and his wife's inheritances, investments, book royalties, and financial gifts from his father. When younger, Darwin had been attracted to the clergy largely because being a parson of a rural parish would give him ample time to follow his naturalist and geological interests.

There had been rumors during the first part of the association's meetings that evolution would be debated during the Zoology Section's sessions. Many persons attended these meetings in the expectation of witnessing intellectual fireworks (Desmond, 1997: 276). During Thursday's session, Huxley defended an attack on evolution by comparing brain structures of apes and humans. On Friday, Huxley also presented a paper on the embryonic development of sea squirt eggs. The stage was set for a more emotional confrontation on Saturday.

Saturday's Zoology Section meeting drew such a large crowd of an estimated 700 to 1,000 persons that the venue was shifted to a larger meeting room. These included university officials, students, anti-evolution clergy, amateur naturalists, and members of the general public. In addition to university officials, the most famous personage in attendance was Bishop Samuel Wilberforce whose administrative responsibilities included the town and University of Oxford. He was also vice president of the British Association hosting the annual conference.

Wilberforce was a famous orator. He was known by the nickname "Soapy Sam" because of his rhetorical skills enabling him from being pinned down to specific points during debates. He would be nicknamed "Slippery Sam" or "Slick Sam" today. He was conservative and anti-evolution, though not familiar with the latest biological discoveries supporting evolution. Wilberforce sat on the stage because of his fame and prestige although he was not officially scheduled to speak. He was, however, prepared to present his views criticizing evolution and had the evening before discussed with a friend what he might say. A number of participants delivered comments against Darwinism during the first part of the session and members of the audience began to shout for Wilberforce to also present his views.

Wilberforce began his presentation by criticizing Darwin's *The Origin of Species*. Ignorant of the fine points of Darwin's theory, Wilberforce relied on sarcasm and humor to ridicule Darwin and other works on evolution (Irvine, 1955: 6). The session had been going on for two hours in a stuffy room when Wilberforce tried to break the audience's tension by asking Huxley whether apes originated on his grandfather's or grandmother's side of the family (Desmond, 1997: 278). Huxley saw his chance to win the debate because Wilberforce had committed an ungentlemanly act: he had openly suggested sexual behavior—essentially bestiality—in public with gentlemen and ladies in attendance. This act was a serious breach of etiquette since gentlemen with independent incomes dominated science at that time. They and their audiences expected science to be presented in a dignified manner free from obscenities. While students and those who were politically radical (supporting evolution as a rationale for their political agenda) may have enjoyed the ribald reference, others considered the mention of sex between a gentleman's (Huxley's) grandparent and an ape in very bad taste.

Huxley responded not with scientific facts but with a lesson in good manners. The response by Huxley is worth quoting at length. Huxley (Desmond, 1997: 279) began his response with barely controlled anger and said he:

> ...had listened with great attention to the Lord Bishops [sic] speech but had been unable to discern either a new fact or a new argument in it—except indeed the question raised as to my personal predilection in the matter of ancestry—That it would not occurred to me to bring forward such a topic as that for discussion myself, but that I was quite ready to meet the Right Rev.

prelate even on that ground. If then, said I the question is put to me would I rather have a miserable ape for a grandfather or a man highly endowed by nature and possessed of great means of influence and yet who employs these faculties and that influence for the mere purpose of introducing ridicule into a grave scientific discussion, I unhesitantly affirm my preference for the ape.

There is no official account of the proceedings and witnesses' accounts vary in many details. While at least one lady fainted from the excitement of the debate—perhaps from the heat—members of each side thought each had won the debate. Witnesses on both sides of the debate were clear the Bishop was not acquainted with the latest scientific findings supporting evolution. This lack of scientific knowledge among creationists was even more apparent during the Scopes trial of 1925 in Dayton, Tennessee.

The Scopes Trial

The first major public confrontation during the twentieth century between creationists and evolutionists occurred in Dayton, Tennessee in 1925. The state legislature had passed the Butler Act on March 21, 1925 making it (Gould, 1983: 64):

unlawful for any teacher in any of the Universities, Normals and all other public schools of the state and all other public schools of the state—which are supported in whole or in part by the public school funds of the State, to teach any theory that denies the story of the Divine Creation of man as taught in the Bible, and to teach instead that man has descended from a lower order of animals.

A significant feature of the Butler Act was that, unlike earlier anti-evolution measures passed in other states, Tennessee's law made the teaching evolution a crime punishable by a fine (Numbers, 1998: 77). The American Civil Liberties Union (ACLU) had advertised for someone willing to challenge the constitutionality of this anti-evolution statute soon after it was enacted. The advertisement read in part (Larson, 1989: 58):

We are looking for a Tennessee teacher who is willing to accept our services in testing this law in the courts. Our lawyers think a friendly test can be arranged without costing the teacher his or her job. Distinguished counsel have volunteered their services. All we need is a willing client.

Dayton's leaders decided a trial dealing with the evolution-creationism issue would give the town's economy a boost (Webb, 1994: 85) and they asked Scopes to volunteer to challenge Tennessee's anti-evolution law. The civic leaders did not expect that hundreds of reporters would converge on Dayton and make the city a symbol for intolerance and intellectual backwardness. Each side was confident it could convince its opponent of the correctness of its own arguments (Smout, 1998) and wanted to present its case to the courts and the public.

John Thomas Scopes was a football coach and general mathematics and science teacher who had briefly taught biology as a substitute teacher. Scopes had not lectured on evolution but he had assigned a state-approved textbook containing material dealing with evolution. Scopes could not recall ever teaching evolution and this uncertainty kept him from being a witness in his own defense.

The eight-day trial, especially the debates during the seventh day, took on heroic proportions. The trial was as closely followed in 1925 as was O. J. Simpson's trial in 1995 and no newspaper or magazine in the United States ignored the event. The trial became a watershed in the creationist strategy to include their view in school curricula. Creationists had not realized before the Scopes trial how well established evolutionary contents were in public schools nor did they realize how much in the minority their views were among educators and scientists.

William Jennings Bryan (1860–1925) volunteered to prosecute Scopes although he had not argued in court in decades. Bryan, as has been noted, was alarmed by what he saw as the growing atheism and the sinfulness of the American public. He was spending his retirement years delivering lectures to fundamentalists on the need for a moral renewal. He had expressed his opposition to evolution in his 1904 speech *The Prince of Peace*, which he had delivered to enthusiastic audiences for decades. Bryan was convinced evolution rejected the Biblical description of creation, which led in turn to atheism, lawlessness, and the growing militancy in Germany. Bryan also felt the argument that humans are descended from monkeys was as invalid as the argument that monkeys were a form of degenerate humans (Levine: 1965: 261).

Bryan became increasingly anti-evolution. In 1921, Bryan, delivered his lecture *The Menace of Darwinism*, which was published in pamphlet form and read widely by religious conservatives. It made Bryan the spokesman for anti-evolutionists. In *The Menace*, Bryan attacked evolution for destroying morality and Christian values, including a belief in immortality. He ended the lecture with (Levine, 1965: 264), "Darwinism is not science at all; it is a string of guesses strung together. There is more science in the twenty-fourth verse of the first chapter of Genesis...than in all that Darwin wrote...[Darwinism] requires more faith in CHANCE than a Christian is required to have in God." These accusations remain the major arguments contemporary creationists make against evolution. In 1924, Bryan delivered another popular speech, *The Origin of Man*, in which evolution was described as a poison to religion and society. He also rejected theistic evolution as a philosophy that eliminates God as an active creator and historical presence (Smout, 1998: 49–50).

Though past his prime as a public speaker, Bryan was at the time of the Scopes trial America's best and most well known orator. His presence ensured not only spectacular rhetoric but the national recognition an important trial was taking place. Bryan's speeches during the trial were made with his back to the judge to better address the spectators and reporters; he knew his audience expected rhetorical fireworks and they were not disappointed. His speeches and the expert testimony presented to the Court in writing were published in newspapers throughout the United States.

Clarence Darrow and Dudley Field Malone headed the defense team. Darrow, an aggressive Chicago lawyer and admitted agnostic who reveled in courtroom dramatics, was the most famous defense attorney of the time. He specialized in defending labor and political radicals of the time. He was also a popular lecturer defending workers' rights, pacifism, and academic freedom. He had just successfully defended Loeb and Leopold. The general public viewed the reduction of their sentences from execution to life imprisonment as a miscarriage of justice (De Camp, 1968: 89).

Malone was also a well-respected lecturer on civil rights. Like Darrow, Malone wanted to defend the right to teach evolution without interference from those with a religious agenda. He was known primarily as a divorce lawyer, and the ACLU officials were not pleased when Malone offered his services in part because he was a lapsed Catholic as well as a non-southerner.

Pre-trial consultations among Scopes, ACLU representatives, and Darrow established the general strategy for the trial. The defense team would challenge the teaching of creationism in the schools but allow Scopes to be found guilty of violating the Butler Act. The aim of the defense was to carry an appeal to higher courts and eventually present the case to the U. S. Supreme Court (Levine, 1965: 327–8). Other state legislatures had already or were planning to pass anti-evolution laws, and ACLU officials wanted to strike down all of these laws at one time through a decision by the U. S. Supreme Court that could not be further challenged.

Unexpectedly, members of each side believed their opponents presented a better argument and won its case. Creationists were especially galvanized by the

Scopes trial because they believed their cause to be threatened and perhaps lost. Bryan's death five days after the end of the trial made him both a martyr and a rallying point for creationists. As a result of the Scopes's trial, alarmed creationists increased their efforts and twenty-three anti-evolution bills were introduced in state legislatures, a number larger than before the trial (Numbers, 1998: 88).

Leading scientific creationist Henry M. Morris reflects the typical creationist view that the trial was unfairly won by evolutionists and somehow the weaknesses of the evolutionary argument were once again ignored. Morris (1993:76) represents those creationists who continue to believe evolution has no real defense:

> The real poverty of the evolutionists' scientific position, however, could have been evident to anyone who would take the trouble to read the actual trial transcripts. The poverty of evolutionism has also been repeatedly reemphasized over the past half-century by the perpetual stream of books, articles, and other replays of the Scopes trial. It was evolution's great triumph (greater even than the famed Huxley-Wilberforce debate), and evolutionists never seem to have anything better to offer when there arises a need to defend evolution.

Bryan's arguments during the trial were the weaker in some respect. He acknowledged that selected Biblical passages were to be understood as symbolic. Bryan also admitted he not an expert in scripture and made several errors dealing with the Bible's contents. However, many anti-creationists felt Darrow's too-aggressive style did more harm than good for the cause of evolution. Each side in the trial had cause for both celebration and embarrassment in the choice of spokespersons. Bryan also presented the argument used today that taxpayers had the right to "control the schools which they *create* and *support*..." He viewed teachers as servants of the state and of the local boards of education, and they should teach what local taxpayers wanted taught (Levine, 1965: 331). While this position reflected his reformist and populist values, the courts have consistently disagreed that members of local school boards have the authority to include religious material in the curriculum.

Darrow's central legal argument was that the Butler Act violated the constitutional principle of separation of state and religion and the act was an attempt by fundamentalist Protestants to insert their religious views into an educational curriculum (Webb, 1994: 87). This argument became standard throughout the rest of the century and continues today (De Camp, 1968: 131–2; Ginger, 1958) as the major argument against the inclusion of creationist material in public schools. For their part, creationists have used the scientific creationist arguments that (A) evolution and creationism are equally true; (B) scientific creationism is a scientific and not a religious argument; (C) evolution has been proven to be false; and (D) it is unfair not to expose students to arguments showing the weaknesses of evolutionary models. Goals A and C may seem incompatible but one or the other had been used when the strategy seemed appropriate. Anti-evolutionists are likely to tell their audiences evolution has been proven false while in the courts, they are likely to argue evolution and creationism are equally matters of faith. Contemporary creationists' major goal is to include creationist material in school curricula. Failing that goal, creationists wish to exclude evolutionary material from textbooks and lectures.

Scopes was found guilty (after the jury deliberated for nine minutes) of violating the Butler Act—the bill banning the teaching of evolution—and the judge fined Scopes $100. However, upon appeal, it was announced the judge did not have the authority to levy fines more than $50 and the Tennessee Supreme Court overturned the verdict. The hopes of the defense of taking the case on further appeals ultimately to the U. S. Supreme Court were dashed and the case ended on a whimper. In his conclusion, defense lawyer Clarence Darrow asked the jury for a guilty decision so he could, in fact, make a later appeal. The Butler Act was repealed in 1967 though it had remained ignored since 1925. Another anti-evolution bill was passed by the Tennessee legislature in 1973 (Gould, 1983: 273). The 1973 bill demanded equal time for evolution and creation and stated that evolution be described in a textbook attachment as "…not represented to be a scientific fact." This declaimer reflects a new strategy by scientific creationists discussed in the fourth chapter.

Consequences of the Scopes Trial

Fascination with the trial and its results continues to the present. A Broadway play and 1960 Academy Award-winning film *Inherit the Wind* with Spencer Tracy as Darrow and Frederic March as Bryan renewed interest in the issue a generation after the 1925 trial. Curiously, both creationists and evolutionists recommend the film to their separate audiences. A second production of *Inherit the Wind* was produced during 1988 with Jason Robards as Clarence Darrow and Kirk Douglas as Williams Jennings Bryan.

The organization *People for the American Way* sponsored a reading of parts of the trial's transcript during July 2000. The occasion for the trial's reading was the first anniversary of the decision by the Kansas Board of Education to omit evolution from science testing procedures. The August 1999 decision allowed the teaching of evolution but forbade any such material on the state's examinations.

The result was that teachers could teach evolution if they wished but could not hold students responsible for the material. This was a new strategy allowing creationists to avoid charges of censorship because evolution was not eliminated from the curriculum, nor did the new policy tell teachers what not to teach.

As a result of the Scopes trial, supporters of evolution stereotyped creationists as quasi-illiterate, irrational rustics who could not accept the modern world. Creationists on their part became convinced new approaches for the support of creationism were demanded because their defense lacked intellectual respectability. Bryan's defense had been based on the scriptures while his command of scientific facts was based on outdated information easily demolished by Darrow. Creationists also began to attempt the introduction of creationism in science classes rather than the exclusion of evolution.

The Scopes trial forced creationists to reconsider their strategies as well as their goals. Anti-evolutionists still attempted to influence state legislatures. Creationists also began to focus their attention on local boards of education, where local community members, many of whom were also church members, were more likely to hold views sympathetic toward creationism. More attention was also placed on attacking textbooks that included evolutionary material. The trial also encouraged creationists to form more united fronts. Many creationists assumed evolutionists formed a well-organized conspiracy and the proper response was to also form coalitions (Livingstone, 1987: 158).

In addition, the trial forced a more antagonistic dichotomy between those who accepted some form of Darwinism and those who did not. Before, many persons felt evolution and religion could accommodate each other. Bryan was representative of the attitude that evolution for all but humans was acceptable and various types of creationism were equally acceptable. Now, however, a stricter line was drawn between evolutionists and Young-Earth creationists. An accommodation that had lasted for almost a century now ended, and it became more difficult for fundamentalists to be theistic evolutionists or even Old-Earth creationists.

The majority of the United States public viewed fundamentalists as those who had exchanged for their intellect a narrow faith. Fundamentalists were pictured as anti-intellectuals with stunted minds. As a result of this negative image, Protestants who focused their attention on the book of Genesis rejected the terms "fundamentalists" and increasingly called themselves "creationists." In the seventies, the term "scientific creationism" became common; in the nineties, creationists introduced the term "intelligent design." These terms, however, refer to creationists, usually those who believe the universe is roughly six to ten thousand years old.

Creationists also began developing "scientific" evidence for their beliefs. This new strategy, which became dominant in the last decades of the twentieth century, allowed scientific creationists to demand equal time with evolution in the classroom on the principle that scientific creationism was as scientific as evolution; later, more attacks were made to exclude evolutionary material in classrooms on the related principle that evolution was "only" a theory and a matter of faith, as was scientific creationism (Berra, 1990: 133–4). Scientific creationists now present the arguments that creationism is either Biblically based or is scientific whenever it suits their purposes and their audiences.

The 1968 Arkansas Trial

The next significant creation-evolution confrontation occurred in 1968 although there had been other legal challenges since the 1925 Scopes trial. Twenty southern states passed anti-evolution statutes after 1925, including Arkansas in 1928. The Arkansas statute made it unlawful for teachers (Thorndike, 1999: 32):

> in any university, college, normal, public school, or other institution of the state, which is supported in whole or in part from public funds derived by state and local taxation, to teach the theory or doctrine that mankind ascended or descended from a lower order of animals…Any teacher or other instructor or textbook commissioner who is found guilty of violation of this act…shall be guilty of a misdemeanor and upon conviction shall vacate the position thus held in any educational institution above mentioned.

In 1965 the official textbook for biology high school courses included a chapter on evolution even though the 1928 Arkansas statute made it illegal for a teacher to "adopt or use in any [educational] institution a textbook that teaches" evolution (Thorndike, 1999: 10). Biology teacher Susan Epperson volunteered to test the Arkansas 1928 anti-evolution statute. Epperson was caught in several dilemmas. She could teach evolution from the official textbook and be found in violation of the statute since the text promoted "the theory about the origin…of man from a lower form of animal." Her contract stated that she was expected to teach all recognized branches of biology, which in her professional view included covering evolution as a topic. Finally, since Epperson believed in the truth of evolution, the Arkansas statute denied her freedom of speech and freedom from unwarranted religious pressures. The dilemma of being expected to teach evolution from a state-selected textbook while she could be fined $500 and lose her job for doing so was also seen as intolerable.

The case went first to the Arkansas Chancery Court. Judge Reed banned all radio, photography and television from his court in order to avoid a well-publicized spectacle. The trial lasted two hours and Judge Reed delivered his decision two months later. Reed issued his opinion that the law was unconstitutional and teaching evolution did not "constitute…a hazard to the health and morals of the community (Larson, 1989: 103)."

Epperson v. Arkansas declared the teaching of evolution legal although the decision had little practical effect in Arkansas and few changed their practices of either teaching or ignoring evolution in their biology classes. The Chancery Court's decision was appealed to a higher court. On June 5, 1967, the Arkansas Supreme Court presented the decision that the anti-evolution statute was constitutional and the law (Livingstone, 1999: 57) was "a valid exercise of the state's own power to specify the curriculum in its public schools." The *Epperson v. Arkansas* case then went to the U. S. Supreme Court and was heard in 1968.

The arguments presented before the U.S. Supreme Court were simple because the Arkansas statute was presented as an attempt by the state to promote a religious view. The Supreme Court Justices declared the anti-evolution statute unconstitutional.

One of the justices, Abe Fortas, had been a fifteen year-old living in Memphis, Tennessee during the 1925 Scopes trial. Fortas had thought at the time Arkansas' anti-evolution law was a disgrace and shamed the state. Fortas issued the Court's unanimous decision, including the following passage (Livingstone, 1999: 97):

> The appeal challenges the constitutionality of the "anti-evolution" statute which the state of Arkansas adopted in 1928 to prohibit the teaching in its public schools and universities of the theory that man evolved from other species of life. The statute was a product of the upsurge of "fundamentalist" religious fervor of the twenties. The Arkansas statute was an adaptation of the famous Tennessee "Monkey Law" which that state adopted in 1925…The overriding fact is that the Arkansas law selects from the body of knowledge a particular segment which it proscribes for the sole reason that it is deemed to conflict with a particular religious doctrine, that is, with a particular interpretation of the book of Genesis by a particular group.

A dissenting Justice, Hugo Black, noted "this court is prepared to simply write off as pure nonsense the views of those who consider evolution an anti-religious doctrine." Justice Stewart stated that evolution was too "respected" to be excluded from public school curricula (Larson, 1989: 117). The U. S. Supreme Court rejected the legitimacy of scientific creationism as a proper science and creationists would have to look elsewhere for support. The Court also found that the state did not have the right to prohibit teaching of a scientific theory or doctrine to promote a religious doctrine. The Court also found that "the state has no legitimate interest in protecting any or all religions from views distasteful to them (quote in Beckwith, 2003: 12)."

Epperson v. Arkansas established the precedent that banning evolution from schools was tantamount to establishing a religious dimension in school curricula and scientific creationists were forced to change their tactics. The terms "scientific creationism" and "intelligent design" replaced the traditional term "creationism" to support the claim the two terms were as "scientific" as orthodox science.

Scientific creationism would claim after the *Epperson v. Arkansas* decision that scientific creationism and intelligent design were as correct as Darwinism in explaining the variety of life. Both creationist groups would argue the validity of their perspectives apart from Biblical scriptures. Members of scientific creationism and intelligent design also adopted the rhetoric that evolution was based on non-empirical assumptions. Using such an argument, creationists demanded equal time with evolution in schools by using the argument both are equally scientific. Further, scientific creationists began to describe evolution as a theory, meaning it was thought to be tentative and not fully accepted by the scientific community. Because of such arguments, state-sanctioned biology textbooks increasingly contained disclaimers that evolution was "only" a theory and that another alternative explaining biological diversity was available (Livingstone, 1999: 112). Scientific creationists tried to convince various courts, and continue to do so, that the scientific evidence for creationism is as valid, or better, than the evidence for evolution.

In 1982, the Louisiana legislature passed a law stating in part that creation science must be given equal time with evolution. This statute was challenged by the 1987 case *Edwards v. Aguillard.* The decision of the U.S. Supreme Court Judges was similar to that in the 1968 *Epperson v. Arkansas* case. The legal standing of creationism as a religious position was established in the *McLean v. Arkansas* decision during 1982. Judge William R. Overton found creationism did not meet the characteristics of science and that creation science was part of a religious ministry disguised as science. The courts have consistently rejected the introduction of creationism and/or the exclusion of evolution in recent decades as religious attempts at censorship. Attempts to reject evolution or limit its discussion in public schools are now understood to be religiously motivated.

Creationists now focus a large part of their energies at the school board, state, and local levels, and scientific creationists have convinced a number of state education boards to place disclaimers in biology textbooks that evolution was a "controversial" theory not fully established. Meanwhile, biology textbooks devoted less space to evolutionary material than was the case twenty years ago (Witham, 2002: 154). Scientific creationists have gained victories in terms of textbook contents and disclaimers but have consistently lost in the legal courts. Whether the courts will continue to keep creationism material out of high school biology classes is uncertain because of the development of the newest form of scientific creationism: intelligent design (Beckwith, 2002).

Evolution

○ ○
We must never assume that which is incapable of proof.

—*G. H. Lewes*

A major criticism made by scientific creationists is that Darwinism is a materialistic worldview that does not allow for a supernatural force to account for the creation, variety, and development of life. In addition, evolutionists claim the processes of evolution are slow and involve time spans disagreeing with Young-Earth creationists. As a result, scientific creationists reject any evidence supporting the evolutionary perspective. Creationists hope attacking the validity of evolution will result in replacing evolutionary thinking with the Young-Earth creationist model.

Charles Darwin and the Theory of Evolution

The central question for Charles Robert Darwin (1809–1882) was why some plants and animals survived to propagate while most did not. It was obvious to him that the world was not over-populated with organisms, implying their population increases were limited in some ways. He also observed that the physical environments of plants and animals vary due to long-term changes in the weather, earthquakes, and other geological transformations. These changes either force organisms to adapt to new conditions and food sources or the species became extinct. Adaptation is possible because organisms genetically differ from their parents and non-twin siblings. Different genetic traits may offer advantages to be passed on to selected offspring or else the organisms die, do not reproduce, and disappear.

The mechanisms Darwin developed to explain differential survival were natural selection and the principle of differential reproductive success. More offspring are born that can be supported by the current food supply and only a minority survives to produce offspring. The struggle for food and survival is an idea that provided Darwin with the mechanism for natural selection. Darwin found this concept of the continual competition for food in Thomas Robert Malthus's (1766–1834) *An Essay on the Principle of Population* (1798). Malthus stated the birth rate of organisms has the potential to outstrip food supplies. Darwin also observed each offspring was slightly different from its parents. He then hypothesized that some of these differences enabled some animals and plants to survive while other characteristics did not. Animals with a survival advantage have more offspring that those who cannot successfully adapt to this competition for food and other essentials of survival (for an excellent history of the concept of evolution, see Bowler, 1984).

Darwin linked this struggle for food with the need in organisms to adapt to current food supplies and general conditions. An animal that can better escape predators or utilize an unused food source will be more likely to survive and pass these advantages to the next generation. Gradually, these animals or plants increase in numbers and dominate the gene pool to become the majority. This struggle can be within one's own species (in the competition for mates or food), with other species and organisms feeding on the same food sources, or the struggle with predators.

In his major work on evolution, Darwin used the world "evolved" once (the last word in his *Origin*). He preferred the terms "descent with modification" and "natural selection." Other terms, such as the now universally accepted term "evolution," suggest progress or positive change resulting in superior organisms. Darwin was insistent his view of change did not imply progress or superiority. A modification makes an organism more likely to survive and leave offspring; under additional changes, the original modification may become detrimental to survival. Implications of progress resulted in the ideology of Social Darwinism and other forms of social negative comparisons that Darwin would have rejected. We are stuck with the term "evolution," but we must remember that it implies temporary adaptation rather than superiority. Darwin himself noted an adaptation helping a species survive would not remain "superior" should future changing conditions make that adaptation irrelevant.

Two questions that puzzled Darwin and earlier evolutionists were: (1) why so many different species with often minor physical differences existed and (2) why very different animals exhibited similar features (the arm bones of humans and bats, for example, are similar in structure). Darwin's fame as the most significant thinker of his time lies in his placing these and other problems within a materialist evolutionary framework that did not rely on theological statements or religious beliefs as explanations. He also amassed an impressive amount of data supporting his explanations, and, to date, no other framework explains life's diversity in such a convincing manner.

Evolutionary scientists have greatly increased their understanding of evolution since Darwin's lifetime. For example, the science of genetics, as established by Johann Gregor Mendel (1822–84) through his work during the 1860s and rediscovered in 1900, allowed scientists to establish the laws of heredity and the transmission of traits. There is now also more acceptance of the role random mutations play in evolution. In addition, fieldwork has shown that divisions of a species through geological accidents, migration, etc, have significant roles in speciation. The discoveries leading to the understanding of DNA and molecular level studies show that neutral mutations and genetic drift are also important evolutionary mechanisms (Patterson, 1999). However, the basic mechanism of natural selection remains unchallenged in its ability to explain and predict.

Scientific creationists are forced from numerous examples to recognize that adaptation and mutation take place. They now separate microevolution from macroevolution, accepting only the former as a possibility. Creationist and retired physicist Lee Spetner explains adaptation due to environmental changes as built into organisms by a creator. A changing environment triggers adaptations that are (Spetner, 1998: 183–84):

> nonrandom variation[s] that could lead to observed evolution. These mutations may act as switches triggered by the environment that switch the genome to one of a preexisting set of potential states to produce an adaptive phenotype…My suggestion here is speculative. We do not yet have an example of a mutation that is sufficiently well understood on the molecular level that we can see (1) just how the environment triggers it and (2) how it produces a phenotype adaptive to that same environment.

Spetner is offering a "just-so" story that "could" be feasible, though there is no attempt to explain how many adaptations are pre-programmed in organisms. The evolutionary model is simpler than Spetner's model that cannot be proven or falsified.

The evolutionary model does not assume adaptive possibilities are built into organisms. Instead, offspring that take advantage of new conditions are more likely to survive in greater numbers and produce larger numbers of offspring, which in turn are more likely to survive and prosper. Adaptations emerge in a random manner and most are harmful to the organism, or else they are neutral and offer no reproductive benefit. Harmful and neutral mutations eventually disappear from the gene pool. Positive adaptations are minor because too radical a change tends to be harmful (see Fisher in Ridley, 1997: 112–5). Evolution is a small step-by-step process over a long period of time. Nature has many failures, but every organism is the descendant of generations of accumulations of beneficial adaptations. Fossils indicate the many failures of species to adapt. Natural selection causes the slow accumulation of traits from one generation to the next (Dawkins, 1997).

Evidence of Evolutionary Adaptation

Evolutionists claim that extensive adaptation has taken place in nature and the Biblical belief in the stability of species is contradicted by numerous observations. One example of adaptation is the *Heliothis virscens* moth. It lays its eggs in cotton bolls and the larvae hatch and eat the cotton. Farmers first sprayed DDT on cotton plants in order to destroy the *Heliothis* during the 1940s. The moth population developed resistance to DDT, and stronger and stronger doses were needed (Weiner, 1995: 252). Such adaptations can occur very quickly, and the first case of DDT resistance occurred six years after its introduction (Denholm, Devine, and Williamson, 2002). When DDT was no longer effective against *Heliothis*, farmers began to use pyrethroids. The first recorded resistance was also six years after introduction of the new chemical. In one cotton field, six percent of the moths were resistant to pyrethroids at the start. Four months later, after several moth generations has occurred, sixty-one percent of *Heliothis* had developed resistance to the poison. The adaptation occurred because offspring of resistant parents were more likely to survive to maturity and have offspring themselves.

Another example of microevolution, and therefore (to evolutionists) of macroevolution, is the change of coloration experienced by the peppered moth and other insects in Great Britain and elsewhere. It is also an example of how differently evolutionists and scientist creationists view the same phenomenon. Black and white forms of the moth exist in pepper moth populations. The black form was rare during the first half of the nineteenth century and collectors offered large rewards for them. Collectors marked where and when specimens were found, making it possible to trace the increase of the black moth from 1848 to the present (Weiner, 1995: 272). In the Liverpool area of England, the black moth population in relation to the white peppered moth increased from seven percent to eighty-two percent in thirty-seven years (Grant, 2002).

The records show the white variety became increasingly rare as the black form increased in number until it became the dominant variation. The black form quickly became the majority wherever Britain's surfaces became dark through the pollution from factories. The black form also became dominant in the industrial areas of continental Europe and the United States. Eventually ninety percent of the moths were black rather than white.

The reason for this color change was that these moths spent time on the trunks of trees and underneath the branches. The original white color blended well with the tree's bark and lichen-covered branches and was difficult to spot by predator birds. Black moths were more visible when they landed on tree trunks and were more likely to be spotted, eaten, and leave no offspring. Trees near England's industrial cities soon became covered with soot and grime as the countryside became covered with coal dust. Under such conditions, black moths enjoyed better camouflage and larger numbers survived for longer periods of time. English rural areas not polluted by mills enjoyed higher proportions of white moths; industrial areas contained relatively more black moths. The black variant went from being one in a hundred (or less) in 1848 to more than ninety in a hundred in 1898 (Weiner, 1995: 272). White peppered moths again became dominant after laws regulating pollution from factories were enacted. In West Kirby, England in 1959, before rigorous pollution laws were enforced, black moths accounted for ninety percent of the pepper moth population. This proportion was reduced by 1989 to thirty percent. The black peppered moth, black ladybirds, and dozens of other types of adapted insects are gradually disappearing as their environments become cleaner.

During the 1950s, experimenters raised white and dark moths in laboratories and released them in polluted and non-polluted areas. White moths placed in polluted areas were more likely to be caught by predator birds than their darker counterparts. By contrast, dark moths placed in non-polluted rural areas were more likely to be eaten by birds than paler moths (Patterson, 1999: 51–5). The fate of pepper moths under different environmental conditions demonstrates the power of natural selection.

Scott M. Huse (1997: 147), a creationist and active anti-evolutionist who presents his case in a very sophisticated manner, claims the change in protective color in the peppered moth is definitely not an example of evolution. Huse ridicules the idea that such minor changes support evolution. He states the change of color does not indicate an increasing complexity or a feature not already present in the moth. Huse admits that the moth's changes in distribution of color is an example of "survival of the fittest" in the Darwinian sense but not of evolution and this change from white to black coloration does not illustrate any mechanism leading toward new species. Similarly, Henry Morris (2003: c) defines the coloration changes in moth populations as "variation" and a survival mechanism but not as an example of speciation. Evolutionists on their part insist coloration change due to environmental change *is* evidence that evolutionary mechanisms exist. Huse and Morris are correct when they state no speciation occurred when a moth population changed from primarily white to dark and back again but they do not accept that the change illustrates one mechanism of evolution.

Another critic of the evolutionary model, Jonathan Wells (2000: chapter 7), has developed additional criticisms increasingly used by other scientific creationists in their defense of creationism (see also Milton, 1997: 130–1). Wells states the changes in color observed under different environments are minor and do not reflect evolutionary processes. He also feels the results of the experiments with moths of different coloring were more ambiguous than is generally recorded. Both creationist Wells and evolutionist Patterson (1999) believe the issue is more complicated than has been reported though the latter remains a staunch evolutionist.

There are numerous other examples of differential survival rates due to differences in coloration. The North American field mouse *Peromyscus* varies in coat color. Those *Peromyscus* mice living in sandy soil have lighter color coats than those living where the soil is darker. Field experiments showed owls captured a larger proportion of mice when their coats did not blend with the surrounding. Mice with lighter coats living where the soil is dark are more likely to be caught by owls than those living in sandy, lighter-colored areas (cited in Smith, 1975).

Another example commonly presented as evidence of evolutionary principles is Darwin's finches. Darwin observed there were many species of finches in the Galápagos Islands, some of which were similar to those found on mainland South America. This observation encouraged him to consider how these differences could develop. He rejected the then common creationist belief God placed the different species in the islands for the enjoyment of humanity since the islands were uninhabited. Darwin concluded the multiple species had been formed through evolutionary processes because of the different environments found in and among the islands. Scientific creationist Richard Milton (1997: 150), as do other scientific creationists, disagrees and says the finch groupings are too similar to be considered separate species.

Peter and Rosemary Grant conducted the most thorough series of finch studies in their natural habitat (Weiner, 1995). The Grants observed finches over a number of years in several islands in the Galápagos archipelago. They have conclusively shown how groups of animals change over time under changing conditions by observing these changes as they take place. At one time, a severe drought killed most of the birds living on the Daphne Major Island because the drought resulted in a lack of the most common seeds that provided food. The Grants observed that birds with larger beaks were able to crack seedpods of the caltrop plant, a plant available during the drought, while birds with smaller beaks could not. The effects of small differences in beak size support the Darwinian hypothesis small physical differences are significant to species in response to environmental changes.

The difference in beak size allowing a bird to crack open a caltrop pod was one half of a millimeter. Males with larger beaks were able to survive the drought in larger numbers because they had a food source not available to finches with smaller, weaker beaks. Most of the male finches with smaller beaks either died during the drought or could not find mates. The Grants also showed males with larger beaks were more likely to attract mates because females selected big-beaked males as mates. This preferential choice for mating is called an "isolating mechanism" in that animals develop behavioral habits keeping emerging species separate. A bird may learn a specific song from its parents, for example, and later refuse to mate with a bird with a slightly different call.

Ring Species

Scientific creationists deny changes observed by the Grants and other field researchers show the validity of evolution. They would claim instead small variations within a species, or microevolution, prove only that animals have the innate ability to adjust to changes in their environments. By contrast, while contemporary examples of new species are rare (Strahler, 1999: 397–400), the speciation process is firmly established from the fossil records and is being observed in such phenomena as ring species. Ring species occur when a sub-group becomes separated from the main population and the parts rejoin again at a later date. The two groups can no longer interbreed due to the genetic changes that occurred during their separation. Ring speciation takes place when a species is divided by the formation of a new lake, river, other geologic phenomena, or migration, such as when a subgroup of animals begins to migrate around a lake or mountain in search of more plentiful food supplies. One group interbreeds and gradually becomes different from the other group through genetic drift, mutations, and behavioral changes. When the two groups meet and again share the same geographic area, they are no longer be able to interbreed because of physical differences, including different secondary sexual characteristics such as new color patches or the development of different mating calls that the opposite group does not recognize.

A species of warblers in Tibet gradually dispersed into two separated and isolated groups along the eastern and western sides of the Tibetan Plateau. When the two warbler groups finally met at the northern flank of the plateau, the eastern and western warblers had developed different mating songs unrecognizable to the opposite group. The two groups had become what is known as emerging species, thereby supporting Darwinian principles of physical isolation and sexual selection as mechanisms for genetic changes.

The Herring gull provides another example of speciation in progress through the mechanism of group isolation. The Herring gull ranges around the world near the Arctic Circle. An observer can follow the gull's range by traveling from Great Britain to Canada to Siberia, across Russia, and back to Europe (Ridley, 1985: 5). The North American gulls are physically slightly different from British gulls and the two do not interbreed (Dennett, 1995: 45). The Siberian Herring gulls are now different enough to be called the lesser black-backed gull. One gull now has a bright ring around the eyes, and a fledging bonding with parents wearing the eye rings will not mate as adults with non-ringed gulls. In this case, separation based on distance resulted in genetic isolation and in the development of two distinct species.

Another change caused by natural selection is the concentration of the sickle-cell gene in certain populations. Haemoglobin-S produces sickle-cell anaemia and is caused by a mutant gene. Sickle-cell anaemia is found in central Africa, in the Middle East and India, and in North and Central America (Patterson, 1999: 48). Those who receive the mutation from only one parent lead normal lives and the mutation causes no illnesses. Inheritance of the gene by both parents can cause early death. Those who have the benign form of sickle-cell anaemia are also resistant to malaria. Sickle-cell anaemia is not found in populations traditionally living in areas where there is no malaria. Benign sickle-cell anaemia is a Darwinian adaptation wherever malaria was originally located.

Such genetic changes occur relatively quickly when a subpopulation is isolated. Salmon isolated from their original group adapt in response to their new environment in less than thirty generations. Hendry et al. (2000: 516) separated salmon and transferred a small group from a river to an isolated lake. The new colony showed genetic changes rather rapidly. Speciation thus can proceed quickly once a group is isolated and finds itself in a new environment that can be better exploited with new physical characteristics. Scientific creationists counter that such changes were inherent in the salmon and that the changes are not evidence of evolution. Evolutionists respond that this process, however minor, is evolution itself in action.

Dating Controversies

A major weakness of the scientific creationist position is their insistence the world is between six and ten thousand years old. The geological evidence of a much older earth began to be collected during the early 1800s and has continued through the present. Geologists during the nineteenth century challenged Biblical chronology through the work of Charles Lyell and others, including Charles Darwin. The acceptance of evolutionary thought after Darwin's 1859 publication *The Origin of the Species* was made possible in large part by the evidence of geological time measuring in the millions and, more recently, billions of years. Scientific creationists of the Young-Earth theological school criticize and dismiss all work by orthodox scientists showing dates older than those suggested in Genesis.

The dating arguments between orthodox scientists and Young-Earth scientific creationists are complex and highly technical. This book will ignore most of the debate since it is found in numerous sources from both creationist and evolutionary perspectives and will only consider one dating methodology in detail. The science of geochronology is well established and orthodox scientists have developed a large volume of literature rejecting Young-Earth claims. Studies of ice cores and ocean sediments alone indicate the earth is far older than ten thousand years.

There are currently many ways to measure the age of objects. Radiocarbon dating using varyious techniques is a simple and dependable method and has been used successfully for decades. Maslin and Burns (2000) charted the moisture history of the Amazon Basin for the last 14,000 years through sediment core samples. Sediment samples have also been used to study the growth of the Amazon rain forest over the last 50,000 years (Mayle, Burbridge and Kileen, 2000). Similar core samples have measured temperature variations near the southwest coast of Africa during the last 3.2 million years (Marlow et al., 2000).

The simplest and most reliable dating method is dendrochronology or the measurement of time by using trees. The basis of this methodology is that a tree forms a ring as it grows during each annual growing season. An observer is able to count the rings of a tree section or a core sample and determine the age of the tree. Rings differ in width according to weather conditions and a year of favorable conditions produces a relatively wider ring. A period of unfavorable climate, such as a drought, produces a thinner ring because of less growth (Hitch, 1982: 300).

Leonardo da Vinci (1452–1519) long ago correctly noted this phenomenon could determine past weather patterns.

Harsh years sometime produce no rings and some years may produce two growing seasons and a corresponding two rings. These rare anomalies are easily recognized and taken into account when a tree's lifespan is considered. Scientific creationists such as Henry M. Morris dismiss dendrochronology by stating annual rings overstate the age of trees. This is an incorrect criticism because tree-ring counting is an extremely reliable measure of the age of trees. Since ring profiles in a region are distinctive, an observer can overlap sections to extend the measurements of seasons from living trees to recently dead trees and so on into the distant past. Although scientists have gathered tree genealogies throughout the world, the best tree for analysis by dendrochronologists is the bristlecone pine in east-central California and western Nevada (Ferguson, 1968). The climate where bristlecone pines thrive is dry and this extremely long-lived tree does not rot when dead. The oldest sequences of overlapping bristlecone tree ring patterns have been measured as 7,100 and 8,200 years old (Banninster and Robinson, 1975: 200). Three pines have been dated as more than 4,000 years old and six others as more than 3,000 years old. Another bristlecone pine in Nevada was discovered to be 3,100 years old (Ferguson, 1968).

The problem for Young-Earth creationists is that the oldest trees pre-date both the supposed creation of the earth in 4000 B.C. and the Genesis flood in 2,348 B.C. (Lietha and Byers, 2000: 38). At the very least, the oldest living trees should have been destroyed during the cataclysms accompanying the Genesis flood. Scientific creationist Henry M. Morris states that tree-ring dates are at least twenty percent too old and that the oldest trees are younger than five thousand years and "probably less than 4000 (1985: 193)." Morris does not offer any proof or reference for his dismissal of dendrochronology. In a similar cavalier fashion, scientific creationist Gerald Aardsma dismisses the validity of dendrochronological sequences of trees by his assumption that favorable climatic conditions after the flood caused trees to produce multiple rings (Aardsma, 1993). At the same time, he suggests that if the ring counts are correct, then the flood may have occurred more than 10,000 years ago rather than the common estimate of 4,000 ago. In this manner, scientific creationists deny the evidence of geological time or else make up new "just-so" stories.

Orthodox scientists are convinced the earth is older than ten thousand years and the Darwinian revolution was based on geological evidence of the earth's great age through erosion, raising and falling continents, measurable glacier advances and retreats, and other geological changes. There is evidence, for example, the earth has experienced numerous ice ages in 100,000-year cycles during the past million years (Kerr, 2000; Flannery, 2001: 130). Measurements of ice cores, ocean sediments and changes in the earth's magnetic patterns indicate the earth is much older than ten thousand years.

Physical scientists are convinced that the earth's surface has been formed through very slow processes. A case in point is the sedimentary beds thousands of feet deep. These beds are made up of multiple layers indicating that various types of sediments settled at different times. Geologists estimate some sediments settle at a rate of less than one inch a year, and a thousand feet of sediment can only be the result of much more than the biblical ten thousand years.

The Evidence for Intermediate Fossils

The strongest challenge made by scientific creationists is their demand for evidence of evolution of intermediary fossils indicating a transition from one species to another. Since scientific creationists deny that the earth is billions of years old and insist all fossils were mixed up in different layers during the Noachian flood, they insist fossils do not prove evolution.

Scientific creationists claim there are no intermediate fossils while evolutionists on their part claim that many intermediate forms exist, including the *Archaeopteryx* discussed below. Scientific creationists confuse the issue by stating that intermediate fossils cannot exist because an animal has to be one thing or another. To say that the *Archaeopteryx* is a mixture of reptile and bird is the result of faulty classification. Creationists also note that the *Archaeopteryx* is classified as a bird because of its feathers. If it is classified as a bird, then it cannot be both a bird and a reptile or have reptile characteristics (Gish, 1978: 84 and 1993: 132). Evolutionists strongly disagree.

While there exist numerous examples of speciation and accompanying intermediate forms, one problem faced by taxonomists is that the common classification system does not allow for intermediate forms: an animal or plant, as scientific creationists declare, must be classified into one category or another. David Raup (1983: 157) recognizes this problem that using exclusive categories hides the number of transitional fossils:

> The practicing paleontologist is obliged to place any newly found fossil in the Linnean system of taxonomy. Thus, if one finds a birdlike reptile or a reptile-like bird (such as *Archaeopteryx*), there is no procedure in the taxonomic system for labeling and classifying this as an intermediate between the two classes Aves and Reptilia. Rather, the practicing paleontologist must decide to place

his fossil in one category or the other. The impossibility of officially recogniz-
ing transitional forms produces an artificial dichotomy between biologic
groups. It is conventional to classify *Archaeopteryx* as a bird. I have no doubt,
however, that if it were permissible under the rules of taxonomy to put
Archaeopteryx in some sort of category intermediate between birds and reptiles
that we would indeed do that. Thus, because of the nature of classification,
there appear to be many fewer intermediates than probably exists.

The fossil record includes numerous examples of series indicating the forming
of new species. Though each series is not complete and there exist gaps, camels,
horses, deer, and elephants, to name a few, show specific series of changes. *Titanotheres* are early mammals emerging during the Lower Eocene era as small pig-
sized animals. Through time, *titanotheres* became larger with longer horns and
they developed new species as they grew larger and changed characteristics. The
horns changed position from near the eyes to over the snout (Edwords, 1982: 1)
while the last example of the *titanotheres* has a head a yard long with horns over a
foot long. This progression took over twenty million years and the fossils show a
clear progression of selected features. Creationists cannot argue changes from one
species into another do not exist.

Similar evidence exists in the evolution of the *Protoceratops* into the *Triceratops*
during a twenty-five million years period. The fossils grow in size, number of
horns (from none to three), and strength of jaws. One response of a creationist to
the *Triceratops* sequence is to state that horns can grow larger within the same
"type" of animals and therefore changes in horns are not evidence of evolution
(cited in Edwords, 1982: 9). However, a close analysis of the *Triceratops* shows
drastic physical changes over time no unbiased observer would consider minor.

Additional examples of intermediate forms exist and paleontologists are close
to discovering more complete evolutionary records for a number of animals,
including the modern whale. The ancestors of modern whales were terrestrial
creatures, and there is now available a series of fossils showing the transition of
whales from terrestrial ancestors through intermediate manifestations to their
contemporary forms.

The earliest whale fossil, that of the fifty-two million year old *Pakicetus*, had
teeth similar to terrestrial mammal fossils but a skull more similar to modern
whales than to mammals living at that time. Modern whales have enlarged
sinuses that can fill with blood to equalize pressures while diving (Gould, 1995:
363). The skull of *Pakicetus* does not have space for these sinuses and therefore
could not dive deeply. Its range was former river deltas and shallow coastlines
where in fact its fossils have been located. Unlike modern whales it had teeth that

were effective for catching fish (Wade, 1998: 145). *Pakicetus* also did not have the directional hearing to allow it to hear underwater as do modern whales. Modern whales hear for the most part through their jaws as sound vibrations go from the jaw to a fat pad and then to the middle ear (Gould, 1995: 364). *Pakicetus* had no space for fat pads and its hearing mechanism was similar to that of its land-based ancestors. It is obvious that *Pakicetus* had intermediate features that belonged to both ancient land-based mammals and modern whales (Strahler, 1999: 441).

Another early whale, the *Basilosaurus*, had hind legs that were too small to propel it in water. Its legs in this case were vestigial features. *Ambulocetus natans*, another pre-contemporary whale, weighted an estimated six hundred pounds and was the size of a sea lion (Gould, 1995: 367). It had large powerful legs, a hoof at the end of each toe, and no horizontal tail fluke as do modern whales. It was roughly eight feet long and lived fifty-five million years ago. *Ambulocetus* swam by both flexing its spinal column as do modern whales and by paddling with its large feet, making the creature a true intermediate animal (Wade, 1998: 145). Another characteristic of some contemporary whales is their ability to grow teeth that do not break the surface of the gums and are never used for feeding. Evolutionists define these vestigial teeth as evolutionary evidence that whales' ancestors had teeth. Another argument for whales' mammalian ancestry is the fact that they swim using a vertical up-and-down spinal movement, as do terrestrial mammals such as otters and humans. By contrast, fish move through water by flexing the back halves of their bodies in horizontal side-to-side movements.

The case of *Archaeopteryx* (meaning "ancient wing") best illustrates the conflicting worldviews of evolutionists and scientific creationists. The *Archaeopteryx* lived 150 million years ago and is so far the most ancient bird fossil as yet discovered. Evolutionists define the fossils of the *Archaeopteryx* as a convincing intermediary organism as well as the oldest discovered creature with feathers. The seven fossils and one fossilized feather are unusually complete in great detail, including fine imprints of true feathers on both the forearms and legs. The three complete specimens contain the same characteristics. Evolutionists point to the fact that *Archaeopteryx* had both reptilian and birdlike features. It was about three feet long with teeth in its jaws, a long bony tail, and true feathers. However, the *Archaeopteryx* is dismissed as a simple bird by scientific creationists because of its feathers. It is nonetheless a true intermediate because it had both bird and reptile features.

It is unclear whether this reptile-bird flew or glided, though the current consensus is that *Archaeopteryx* flew to some extent because its feathers were asymmetrical in the same manner as the feather construction of modern flying birds (flightless birds have symmetrical feathers). The claws were curved indicating the bird could perch on branches to use as a platform to achieve at least modified flying and soaring (Shipman, 1998: 135). Other researchers feel the fact that it had a sternum to anchor muscles used in flight suggests the ability to fly. The shape of the shoulders also suggests that the *Archaeopteryx* could fly. *Archaeopteryx* probably descended from theropod dinosaurs because theropods are bipedal and the front appendages could evolve into true wings. Its ancestor developed feathers before flying became possible since feathers provide insulation and make the wearer more difficult to catch.

The *Archaeopteryx* had feathers and a fused wishbone like modern birds. A fused wishbone is important because it allows birds to fly and breathe at the same time. The creature also had a relatively small brain, long tail, and separate hand bones like reptiles (though its brain was larger than its reptilian ancestors). The pelvis and feet are reptilian rather than bird-like. The skeleton and skull are reptilian. The shapes and proportions of the *Archaeopteryx's* bones resemble its presumed dinosaur ancestors more than do the bones of modern birds. It also had lizard-like teeth with a bird-like beak. The bones were hollow suggesting an ability to fly or at least to soar due to decreased weight.

Further evidence for the reptilian origin of contemporary birds is the finding it is possible to induce chickens to grow teeth, as did their reptilian ancestors, by inserting on the gums of chick embryos tissue taken from the teeth area of mouse embryo (McGowan, 1984: 121). This suggests birds maintain the ability to grow teeth but are no longer able to activate the appropriate gene. It is also possible to force chickens to grow scales instead of feathers on their legs (as did their ancestors) by genetic manipulation.

Although the ancestry of the *Archaeopteryx* is as yet unknown and its links with modern birds have not been established, recently discovered fossils in China of later, intermediate animals capable of flight also show bodily structures similar to modern birds. The *Hesperornis* had teeth and thick bones but its general form was much like a modern bird (Rich et al., 1996). The *Hesperornis* is one of thirteen types of similar fossils with both reptilian and bird-like features. Scientific creationists cannot claim with any validity that mixed, intermediate forms of birds do not exist. Future excavations in China will probably unearth additional forms of animals with mixed reptile-bird features capable of flight.

Fossils of birds living earlier than the *Archaeopteryx* suggest how feathers developed. The *Protopteryx* is one of the most primitive bird fossils available for study. Its tail feathers are scale-like and do not branch out as feathers do in modern birds. Evidence from *Protopteryx* remains and other fossils suggests feathers developed first as elongated scales, a central shaft later developed, then other features developed to result in contemporary feathers (Zhang and Zhou, 2000). A variety of types of feathers are found in the wings of penguins. Some are scales, some are fully developed feathers, and others exhibit intermediate characteristics of both scales and true feathers. Variations within one animal suggest how feathers developed from scales to contemporary feathers. Both feathers and scales are formed from a horny protein called keratin and it is easy to hypothesize how keratin scales developed into feathers with intermediate forms being useful to the animal.

The *dromaeosaur* was recently discovered in fine-grained deposits that preserved unusually detailed imprints of feathers from over all of its body. The 130-million-year-old *dromaeosaur* resembled a duck with a three-foot reptilian tail. Its short arms could not have allowed it to fly. Its three forward-pointing toes resemble those of modern birds but the *dromaeosaur* is otherwise reptilian. The *dromaeosaur's* back carried primitive forms of feathers while its front limbs sported more modern types of feathers (Wilford, 2001).

Paleontologists do not yet completely understand the evolution of birds and their origins although the dinosaur-to-bird link is now widely accepted. Paleontologists have begun to trace the patterns of bird evolution where before little was known of the paths from dinosaur to modern bird. A more modern fossil 80 million years old, the *Asparavis*, is offering clues on the more recent ancestry of birds. *Asparavis* has 27 physical features that are similar to modern birds and 12 traits belonging to earlier bird types. It is difficult to determine whether certain other fossils are flightless birds or feathered dinosaurs such as the *Sinosauropteryx*. Many of these fossils exhibit mixtures of primitive and modern features scientific creationists cannot explain (Stokstad, 2001).

Human Evolution

Scientific creationists consistently reject evidence of evolution based on studies of hominid fossils. John Ankerberg and John Weldon are typical when they state (Ankerberg and Weldon, 1998: 245):

> …the popular belief expressed by evolutionists, and widely believed by the public, is that the hominid fossil evidence proves human evolution. *Nothing could be further from the truth.* Not only does it not prove human evolution, it actually disproves it and strongly offers evidence for divine creation.

One of the most well-known evolutionary link to contemporary humanity is Lucy, whose remains were discovered by Donald Johanson in the Olduvai Gorge in Tanzania (Johanson and Shreeve, 1989). Lucy, 40% of whom was recovered, was a member of *Australopithecus afarensis* living roughly three million years ago. One location contained the partial remains of an estimated thirteen or more individuals (Tattersall, 1998: 113). *A. afarensis* was extremely dimorphic with males much larger than females. *Homo sapiens* exhibit a roughly twenty percent dimorphism, much less than Lucy's species. Lucy's dimorphism is more similar to that found among present-day gorillas than *Homo sapiens*, whose male-female differences in size are relatively slight.

Australopithecus afarensis males weighed an estimated one hundred pounds and females about-sixty-five pounds (Tattersall, 1998: 114). Lucy stood about 3 ½ feet tall. *A. afarensis* composite skulls (few complete skulls survive burial of millions of years) have general apelike proportions, including large jaws, and small brains but with small teeth with modern features. Contemporary human teeth are covered with a thick coat of enamel while primates' teeth are not. Lucy's canine teeth are smaller than that of modern apes' but larger than those of *Homo sapiens*. The most important feature of *A. afarensis* is that they walked upright as do modern humans. This important feature places *A. afarensis* firmly in the human classification.

Paleoanthropologists hypothesize hominids became able to walk upright, ventured into the savannahs, and began to eat more grasses and grains. This change of diet would result in their large teeth becoming less useful. As succeeding generations selected for smaller, more useful teeth, they lost their ape-like dentition. The ability to walk upright on two feet offers the chance to travel for longer periods in the search for food. The ability to stand upright also allows for better observation of possible prey and predators. Walking upright also frees the hands to carry supplies making longer journeys possible to reach additional food supplies (Ruse, 1982: 241–6). The leg and hip structures of *A. afarensis* show they were capable of walking upright. Chimps and gorillas have bony ridges near the base of their fingers as a result of knuckle walking. They curl their fingers and place the second segment of their fingers on the ground when they walk. This action forms a ridge on the fingers to help keep the wrists rigid and better support the body's weight. Contemporary humans do not have this ridge, nor did *A. afarensis*. Lucy therefore walked upright in a manner very similar to modern humans (Stokstad, 2001).

More significant clues are found in Lucy's, and her relatives', knees and leg bones. The knee joints and shinbones indicate Lucy and kin walked upright (Tattersall, 1998: 115). Pelvis and lower leg bones also indicate upright posture. Lucy's spine was double-curved thereby indicating she could walk upright for long periods without discomfort, though probably with a different gait from that of *Homo sapiens*.

In spite of these similarities, Lucy and her relatives looked different from modern humans. They had longer arms and shorter legs in relation to their height. Hands and feet curved, indicating the older ability to grasp when on tree branches, a feature that is a holdover from a tree-dwelling past. *A. afarensis* could live comfortably in trees for long periods of time and were also able to venture into the savanna for additional sources of food. Some contend the major change in evolutionary development in humanity's ancestry is not a large brain but the ability to stand upright. The evidence shows *A.* afarensis was a being with significant *Homo sapiens* as well as apelike characteristics

A. afarensis is not a direct ancestor of *Homo sapiens*. It is important to conceptualize evolution as taking a bush pattern rather than a ladder. The ladder-type model of evolution implies a step-wise process in which one change leads to another. Each "rung" is an intermediate step from one generation to another. The process of evolution is better conceptualized as a bush with many branching and dead ends. *A. afarensis* is a branch rather than a direct ancestor of modern humans since it became extinct before *Homo sapiens* evolved. Lucy is not a "missing link" because she was closer in physical characteristics to modern humans than to primates.

The Creationist Response

Scientific creationists have rejected what orthodox scientists consider as proofs of evolution. Scientific creationists first deny dating procedures indicating organic remains, such as fossils, are older than six to ten thousand years old. Below are the responses of scientific creationists to claims of speciation in general and to the nature of the *Archaeopteryx* in specific.

The struggle for resources among organisms would not concern scientific creationists since many are willing to admit that contemporary animals struggle for survival and adapt slightly to changing external conditions. However, Darwin was interested in competition among animals and plants because he wanted to explain why there existed so many different species in the modern world and in the past. Naturalists estimate that there are more than five million different species, though 1.5 million species have so far been classified. Even in Darwin's day, scientists had discovered a large number of extinct and living species suggesting a large amount of change had taken place among living organisms. These findings disturb creationists because fossils suggest many of God's creations must have been imperfect for their descendants to need to change. Creationists also object to the Darwinian principle that animals change over time to develop new species. Creationists insist God originally created all life and further differentiation is both impossible and non-Biblical.

There are many examples of organisms adapting to new conditions, and creationists now accept the fact of microevolution, or changes within species. Most nineteenth century creationists believed animals did not change from generation to the next since that suggested continuing creation. Darwin, in his *The Origin of Species*, presented numerous examples showing the concept of a static nature was contrary to evidence. Darwin showed conclusively that changes had occurred in domestic animals and others. Scientific creationists now accept the fact of microevolution but are adamant the processes making microevolution possible cannot evolve new species.

Creationists state animals were born as "kinds," and each has the potential for some change, as when humans develop new strains of cattle, dogs, or cats. This is why Noah did not have to take two of each subspecies of felines. One generic feline pair could produce the lions, tigers, domestic cats, etc. in existence. However, creationists believe making the mental leap from micro- to macroevolution demands a leap based on faith rather than data. Evolutionists maintain the processes making microevolution possible are also valid in macroevolution: there is no difference between the two except degree.

The issue of speciation is further significant because scientific creationists believe there were no deaths before the expulsion of Adam and Eve from the Garden of Eden. This means all fossils were formed during the two thousand years between the expulsion and the Genesis flood. Paleontologists estimate that the fossil evidence suggests that at least fifty million species have become extinct (Ross, 1998: 151). Scientific creationists have not explained in detail why so many different species are found in the fossil record and among contemporary life.

Scientific creationists such as Scott Huse claim an intermediary creature is impossible. As we have seen, scientific creationists reject the possibility that birds could have evolved from dinosaurs. Huse adds the criticism that an intermediate form of early birds could not have existed because it would have lungs with both reptilian and bird-like features. The notion of an animal with both bird-like lungs in the shape of tubes and reptilian air sacks is "totally inconceivable (Huse, 1997: 150)." It is unlikely that *Archaeopteryx* had a mixture of two types of lungs. Unfortunately, soft tissues such as lungs and hearts rarely fossilize and the issue remains unresolved.

Duane T. Gish provides the most detailed criticisms of fossil evidence of evolution; his writings provide the basis for most of the comments on fossils made by other scientific creationists. Gish insists *Archaeopteryx* is completely a bird. Nor does he believe a creature with bird-like hips could have emerged from a reptilian ancestry (1995: 133). Furthermore, Gish argues some reptiles have long tails while some do not and other modern birds have claws, as did *Archaeopteryx*. He notes that the South American Hoatzin has two characteristics defined as reptilian though it is a bird in all other features (Gish, 1995: 85). However, these two reptilian features are ambiguous at best since the Hoatzin has a keel but a small one, and only juveniles have claws on their wings. Evolutionists would define the Hoatzin either as a mosaic (one with mixed features) or as a "living fossil," that is, an organism that has not changed since prehistoric times, similar to turtles and crocodiles. The claws of the Hoatzin juveniles are seen as a survival of an earlier stage; the keel is fixed, so it is not a true reptile. Gish is adept in defining facts to fit his argument in the same way that Henry M. Morris (Morris 1984: 85) defines the *Archaeopteryx* as "100 percent bird" while ignoring its reptilian features.

Scientific creationists complain true feathers could not have fully developed at one time (unless designed by a creator) through evolutionary pressures. Feathers probably (scientific creationists are correct in stating such statements are unproven) developed not to make flight possible but to keep the animal warmer and perhaps to provide some protection against the claws of predators. Feathers later provided the capability for short glides (again to escape predators) and then made true flight possible.

Scientific creationist John Kaplan goes further than Huse and Gish in rejecting *Archaeopteryx*. Kaplan, in a research note published in the *Creation Science Quarterly* dismissed the bird-like features of the *Archaeopteryx* by reporting in detail an article published in 1863 by Richard Owen, a person virulently opposed to both evolution and Charles Darwin. Owen found that in only two minor aspects did the fossil resemble a bird. Typical of most scientific creationists, Kaplan (1993) searched the archives until he had found material attacking evolutionary findings, even when such material was more than one hundred years old. It did not occur to Kaplan to conduct his own research or to investigate more recent analyses of the structure of *Archaeopteryx*. Kaplan's "research" is typical of the research, or lack of research, characterizing scientific creationists.

Creationists have focused considerable resources in their attempts to dismiss fossil evidence of evolution. Arthur C. Custance (1972 [1959]: 160) argues that:

It is well known that the human skull is plastic enough that it may, *in the adult stage*, be modified towards a more apelike form if the eating habits of the ape are simulated in one way or another by man...Such deformation can occur within a single lifetime. It is, of course, not inherited by the offspring, but if the conditions of life persist over several generations, chances are that a few skulls will be preserved as fossils whose configuration might give the impression that their owners were not far removed *by descent* from an apelike subhuman ancestor, whereas, in point of fact, no such relationship need be postulated.

Custance states the eating of uncooked foods develops the chewing muscles and bony tissues that appear to belong to intermediate ape-to-human beings. He goes on to compare drawings of an Eskimo head with the head of the "Blue Boy" in Gainsborough's painting. The difference in skull shape is stated to be the result of "the influence of what may be termed a cultured diet" in the latter (Custance, 1973: 162). No reliable evidence exists suggesting particular diets change the musculature of humans to such an extent that two humans would look like members of different sub-species. Nor does Custance offer any evidence human skulls can be "modified toward a more apelike form."

Creationists also point to on-going discoveries of human or proto-human fossils that force archeologists to revise their timetables and genealogies. They assume that any change "proves" evolution has been falsified. Instead, new discoveries add to knowledge. It is now known that different species of humans and earlier forms of humanity lived at the same time, as did the Neanderthals and *Homo sapiens*. Ongoing discoveries do not "disprove" evolution but rather add support to the existence of the complexity of evolutionary processes.

Scientific Creationism

○ ○
Fish don't walk and Jesus still lives.

—bumper sticker

Introduction

Scientific creationists now lead creationists in presenting creationism to the public and the courts and also in attacking evolution. This chapter presents the major arguments made by scientific creationists. Instead of relying solely on Biblical sources to defend their positions as creationists did until recent decades, scientific creationists also frame their arguments using scientific terms. Their position is that science as well as scripture proves creationism true and evolution false. Many scientific creationists are familiar with orthodox science and hold graduate degrees in various sciences from secular universities. Scientific creationists also believe that their form of creationism is more scientifically valid than evolution. Scientific creationists respect science in the abstract but believe the majority of scientists have wrongly accepted evolution. As this chapter shows, scientific creationists differ radically from evolutionists in their interpretation of basic facts. In spite of their interests in science, they interpret scientific knowledge within a religious framework.

George McCready and the Start of Scientific Creationism

George McCready Price developed the foundations of scientific creationism during the 1930s. Price was a prolific author of works dealing with religious topics, primarily those dealing with Young-Earth creationism. His writing made possible the emergence of scientific creationism after the Scopes trial in 1925. He ignored whatever did not support his theological beliefs but nevertheless insisted there was empirical support for creationism. Price was careful in his most influential opus to avoid all scriptural supports for his belief in a worldwide Genesis flood. He is typical of creationists who begin with the assumption a worldwide flood occurred although he never admits that this assumption is derived from Biblical scripture.

Price's influential 1935 work, *The Modern Flood Theory of Geology*, gave support to those seeking creationism as a factual alternative to evolution. He begins his argument by assuming that a flood took place and then arranges established, as well as more questionable, scientific evidence to fit his model. This strategy, currently common among scientific creationists, uses plausible interpretations of established data to create the impression there is evidence of a Genesis flood if one were only unbiased. Price took the position, common with contemporary scientific creationists, that if a global flood can be shown to have taken place, then evolution would be proven wrong and creationism the only correct alternative (Price, 1935: 41):

> ...if any such event as a universal Deluge did take place, Lyellism is false, and then the entire scheme of organic evolution must be a blunder.

Price attacked the evolutionists' use of the sequential location of fossils as an index of relative age (older fossils are located in lower strata). Price held the position that fossils were deposited during the global flood causing fossils to be deposited in relation to when they drowned. Price also adopted another strategy still used by today's scientific creationists. Price declared arbitrarily and without external proof that there was no evidence at all of an evolutionary process among organisms (Price, 1935: 81–2):

> Evolution, forsooth! Why, in every case where we can come to actual grips with the facts, there is absolute evidence of degeneracy, not evolution.

The statement above is typical of today's scientific creationists rejection of major parts of established science: they insist in an authoritative manner that evidence of changes in organisms is evidence of a decline caused by sin and post-flood conditions rather than evolutionary processes. The "evidence" Price mentioned is forced, as for example his explanation of why some fossils are larger than their modern counterparts. Decreasing size proved to Price "degeneracy" rather than evolution. Price ignored the fact that the mega-fauna period was actually the result of different climatic conditions from those present today, including warmer seas and a higher atmospheric oxygen content. He rejects contrary evidence with disbelief and ridicule when evidence contradicts his theology. When that strategy fails to convince, Price, typically of scientific creationists, attacks those who disagree with him. Evolutionists are either blind or deceitful (Price, 1935: 106):

> As I have said above, it is quite useless for me to argue with a man who still sticks to the evolutionary scheme of the fossils "from instinct," or *as an act of faith* in some scheme of materialistic philosophy (italics added).

The Major Elements of Scientific Creationism

Henry M. Morris (Morris, 1972, vi-viii) concisely defined scientific creationism in a series of statements including the following:

- The Bible clearly teaches that all things were created in six natural days several thousand years ago, and all other Biblical interpretations of the creation account contain many irreconcilable contradictions with both science and Scripture.

- There is no demonstrated fact of science which cannot be satisfactorily correlated with this simple and straightforward Biblical record...

- No fact of actual observation has ever confirmed the general theory of evolution, as distinct from those minor variations which are known as the special theory of evolution...

- The tremendous complexity and order of the world and its plants and animals can only be explained by intelligent planning, not by a random process of chance variation and natural selection...

- The entire fossil record can be explained better in terms of cataclysmic destruction of all the ecological zones of one age than in terms of evolutionary development of changing worldwide floras and faunas through many ages...

- Belief in special creation has a salutary influence on mankind, since it encourages responsible obedience to the Creation and considerate recognition of those who were created by Him.

- Belief in evolution is a necessary component of atheism, pantheism, and all other systems that reject the sovereign authority of an omnipotent God.

Contemporary scientific creationists argue for the inclusion of Young-Earth creationist material in school science programs on the basis that evolution and creationism are equally matters of faith. However, scientific creationists insist that only their particular form of creationism be included in school science programs. Scientific creationists prefer to ignore other types of creationists as a matter of strategy, though they are most hostile towards theistic evolutionists. Leading scientific creationist Henry M. Morris feels Christian evolutionists are mistaken and heretical in their interpretations of selected Biblical passages. Other scientific creationists are as open in stating their hostility toward other creationists who do not agree with them. For example, Gerard Berghoef and Lester DeKoster (1989) view all varieties of evolutionists as atheists even though many evolutionists insist they hold religious and Biblically acceptable beliefs. In their book *The Great Divide*, the authors believe any form of evolution is a lie constructed by the devil for those who are credulous (Berghoef and DeKoster, 1989). Below are several passages from *The Great Divide* to show their antagonism toward evolution:

- Theistic evolution pays lip service to the omnipresence of God. But its "God" is bound by the "principle of uniformity" which science needs to validate its calculations (p. 29).

- Theistic evolution makes an idol based on its own image by highly selective uses of the Bible. It is repetition of an old blunder (p. 51).

- Christianity **OR** evolution!...It is both man and woman who are the losers as evolution erodes the stability of the family (p. 74).

- The Great Divide is fully exposed now. Christ Himself certifies Genesis. It *is* Christ-ianity **OR** evolution! (p. 152).

The Second Law of Thermodynamics and Its Misuse by Scientific Creationists

A central argument made by scientific creationists is based on a misunderstanding and misrepresentation of the second law of thermodynamics. The second law of thermodynamics states closed systems run down and order (complexity) dissolves into uniformity (entropy) or chaos. Scientific creationists believe the world was perfect until Adam's fall; a perfect order then began to break down as the result of the first couple's sin of rebellion. The presumed end of creation means nothing new can be created, including new species. Henry M. Morris (1977b: 13) states that the laws of science are "laws of conservation and deterioration, not of creation and integration." Morris also supports the scientific creationist claim that only scripture can offer knowledge on creation and creative processes, making the record of creation in the first eleven chapters of the book of Genesis the only reliable form of evidence. Morris summarizes his views on the relationships among creation, science, and the superiority of the scriptures in the following manner (Morris, 1977b: 24):

> We need therefore to recognize plainly that the Biblical "days" of creation were real days, such as we know them today, and cannot possibly be equated with the "ages" of the so-called historical geology. This should not trouble us scientifically, since we have already seen that *science*, as such, is utterly incapable of really telling us *anything* about creation.

The claim by evolutionists that creative processes exist today in nature violates biblical principles and must therefore be rejected in any form, including those statements based on the first two laws of thermodynamics. Evolution cannot be correct since God no longer creates new life forms (Whitcomb and Morris, 1961: 227):

> The plain facts of the situation, therefore, are that evolution has simply *assumed* as the universal principle of change in nature, despite the fact that there is no experimental evidence supporting it and despite the still more amazing fact that universal experience and experimentation have demonstrated this universal principle of change to be its very opposite: namely, that of deterioration!

The law of entropy states that decay of the integrity of a complex system increases as less energy is available to maintain the status quo. The process of entropy causes systems to decrease and prohibit the creation of new forms (Franzen, 1983: 127). The second law of thermodynamics states that while the total amount of energy remains constant, the universe's ability to do work declines as energy becomes equally distributed (entropy). An example of this process is a waterfall. Water at the top of the hill contains potential energy that can be used to operate watermills, etc. By contrast water at the bottom of the fall has dissipated its potential energy and entropy has occurred throughout the waterfall system.

Scientific creationist logic continues that evolution is impossible because if the universe is dying and entropy is increasing, then new life forms are impossible. The process of entropy precludes any creation after the Genesis six-day period and the formation of more complex organisms (Whitcomb and Morris, 1961: 223–7). Henry M. Morris (1985: 43) acknowledges the second law of thermodynamics applies only to closed systems and that there is growth such as the growth of a seed into a tree or the growth of a child into an adult. Morris continues to state that since all systems are open, all must decay. The logic is tortuous but forms the basis of creationists' unique interpretation of the second law of thermodynamics to reject the possibility of evolution. I quote from Henry Morris to show the weakness of his logical structure (Morris, 1985: 43):

> Although it is true that the two laws of thermodynamics are defined in terms of isolated systems, it is also true that in the real world there is no such thing as an isolated system. *All* systems in reality are open systems and, furthermore, they are all open in greater or lesser degree, directly or indirectly, to the energy from the sun. Therefore, to say that the earth is a system open to the sun's energy does not explain anything, since the same statement is true for every other system as well!

Scientific creationists do not explain why development is impossible in some "open" systems and not in others. When I type words into my PC, I am using energy to create words and sentences. I get my energy from food that ate plants or synthesized the sun's energy through photosynthesis. Insisting that all is decaying ignores both scientific reasoning and everyday experience. Anyone who has gotten a burn from lying too long in the sun disproves the scientific creationist position that exchange of energy is impossible. Scientific creationists also ignore the fact local systems can exchange energy on an internal basis, as the sun heats the earth: increased complexity is possible within closed and partially closed systems.

The response to this scientific creationist position is that the second law of thermodynamics applies to closed systems where no energy enters the boundaries. Energy enters the world's system through sunlight. The sun is the energy source allowing living systems to develop (Berra, 1990: 126). Scientific creationists are silent on the effects of the law of entropy when discussing micro-evolutionary changes. If all systems decay toward disorder—or entropy—then changes within species are impossible. Scientific creationists now admit that microevolution, changes within a species, is possible. Henry H. Morris excludes microevolution from the law of entropy (Morris, 1977b: 13) by assuming that intra-species change is not associated with increases in energy use. Other than microevolution, creationists state the evolutionary process violates the second law of thermodynamics because evolution implies increasing complexity, which is impossible according to scientific creationists. Scientific creationists are guilty of ignoring selected facts when it suits them. Evolutionists would also argue that speciation involves change but not necessarily increased complexity.

During the nineteenth century, most creationists believed species were fixed and unchanging. Fossil evidence and Darwin's comprehensive analysis of induced changes in domesticated animals made this position no longer tenable. It is obvious that farmers, dog fanciers, and pigeon collectors have developed new breeds for their own purposes. Anyone attending a county fair or dog or cat show sees how breeders have bred animals and plants to accentuate selected features.

Scientific creationists Wayne Frair and Percival Davis (1994: 74) are more cautious than many scientific creationists in their use of the second law of thermodynamics. They limit the effects of the law of entropy to the creation of life itself. They believe life could not have originated spontaneously and assembled itself to form self-reproductive organisms. Orthodox scientists disagree and theorize that self-reproductive life can emerge using external sources of energy. This view is called *abogenesis* and holds that life emerged from chemical mixtures under specific conditions. These conditions, not yet completely determined, can in theory develop non-living proteins that lead in turn to self-replicative molecules (Birx, 1991: 29). Both micro—and macroevolution refute the creationist's unique interpretation of the operation of entropy.

One possible example of an abogenesis site is the "Lost City" seafloor hot vent. The Lost City vent is located 1,500 miles east of the United States coastline. The water coming out of what are called "hot smokers" is heated by chemical action and contains organic compounds. The Lost City vents exude water heated to 170 degrees Fahrenheit from vents eighty stories tall. Such vents might be similar to conditions allowing life to develop.

Hugo Franzen (1983: 134), professor of chemistry who has taught courses in thermodynamics at the undergraduate and graduate levels, finds that scientific creationists apply twisted, incorrect logic while at the same time ignoring vital fundamentals of the thermodynamic laws. He offers the example of a jar containing hydrogen and oxygen gases in a ratio of two to one. This mixture is a rocket fuel, but the mixture remains inert unless a spark is introduced. The mixture is also stable until platinum is placed in contact with the gases. The hydrogen and oxygen gases will then violently combine to form water.

These chemical reactions are made possible by the introduction of either energy (a spark) or a catalyst (platinum). Creationists ignore the possibility of catalysts and forms of energy making possible new compounds and chemical combinations. DNA, RNA, proteins, and enzymes—the building blocks of life—are such catalysts. Scientific creationists ignore such energy transfers and insist a creator is the only source of fundamental change in nature.

Misuse of the Theories of Louis Pasteur and Theories of the Beginning of Life

Another pseudo-scientific defense presented by scientific creationists is the use of Louis Pasteur's (1822–1895) experiments to show a creator is necessary for the establishment of life. Pasteur made his most important discoveries in the field of bacteriology by showing diseases were the result of bacterial infection rather than supernatural or other non-material causes.

Before his work convinced others, most persons since Aristotle (384–322 B.C.) believed lower forms of life generated spontaneously. People had observed that garbage heaps contained flies and rodents, and it seemed obvious such pests were created by the filth itself. Pasteur demonstrated that this was impossible. He placed pieces of meat in three containers. The first was left open, the second was partially open, and the third was closed tightly. Pasteur demonstrated that after a few days the first bottle contained maggots and eventually flies. The third bottle did not contain any maggots because no flies could enter to lay their eggs on the meat. This established the "life to life" principle used today by scientific creationists and intelligent design supporters.

Evolutionists accept the validity of Pasteur's demonstrations. Pasteur showed life is too complicated to develop spontaneously in a piece of rotting meat though his findings emphatically do not suggest life cannot develop from inert material under certain conditions. Other experiments, by contrast, suggest the building blocks of life originated from mixtures of gasses without the intervention of a creator. Alexander I. Oparin argued during the 1930s that the atmosphere of early earth was filled with a mixture of gasses conducive to the formation of life. Lightning, ultraviolet radiation, and other sources of energy could have transformed these gases into the basic building blocks of life. Stanley Miller and Harold Urey were able to produce under laboratory conditions during 1953 a number of amino acids and other chemicals necessary for life. These and other experiments support Darwin's belief that life could have begun in a "shallow, sun-warmed pond (Ward and Brownlee, 2000: 63–71)."

Evolutionists such as H. James Birx (1991) and scientific creationists such as Henry Morris (1984) are right to point out that the case for a "primal soup" as the origin of life remains unproven though Birx and other orthodox scientists find there exists strong indirect evidence that organisms developed from inert matter. Birx notes that some taxonomists divide life into seven separate primary categories and that each kingdom may have begun independently from the others (Birx, 1991: 34). One problem is that, while the basic elements of life can be produced, no complex molecules with self-replicating capabilities have yet been constructed in laboratories. It is also not clear what the composition of the earth's atmosphere billions of years ago could have been (Casti, 1990) and the issue remains unsolved according to both scientific creationists and evolutionists. The issue of how life started is a weak link in evolutionary arguments though evolutionists are more concerned about how life *developed* rather than how it *began*.

Scientific creationists such as Morris (1984: 232–3) use Pasteur's demonstrations to "prove" life is impossible without supernatural intervention, though that was not Pasteur's conclusion. Pasteur actually showed complex life is not generated from dead organic material. Evolutionists are willing to concede that point although Darwin did not concern himself with the origin of life. The "mystery of mysteries" according to Darwin was the development of new species through natural processes.

The Methodology of Scientific Creationism

The methodology of scientific creationism is limited to making plausible conclusions based on their interpretations of scripture. The *Answers in Genesis* organization, part of the ministry of the *Creation Science Foundation Ltd*, publishes the *Creation Ex Nihilo Technical Journal* to provide a venue for "scientific" publications supporting creationism. *Ex Nihilo* is a glossy journal with superb illustrations and exists because, according to the instructions for authors and supporters, "Christians need to keep on providing scientific answers within a biblical framework, and refining our case (including exposing whatever flaws there may be in old arguments [i.e., evolution])." The format is typical of any technical journal in that each article contains footnotes, diagrams, and references. Most articles contain few or no religious references and the tone is overtly secular, though there are a few articles based on analyses of biblical issues that are similarly formal and academic in style. Some articles are extremely technical and the average reader would have difficulty in following the arguments. The purpose of articles in *Ex Nihilo* is to prove the validity of Biblical passages, often without mentioning that scriptures are the bases for the articles. Most of the references are to other publications in *Ex Nihilo* or other scientific creationist literature, indicating the intellectual isolation of scientific creationism. Authors must accept the following guidelines that are overtly and demandingly religious:

- The Bible is the written Word of God. It is divinely inspired throughout.

- The final guide to the interpretation of Scripture is Scripture itself.

- The account of origin presented in Genesis is a simple but factual presentation of actual events and therefore provides a reliable framework for scientific research into the question of the origin and history of life, mankind, the earth and the universe.

- Scripture teaches a recent origin for man and the whole creation.

- The great flood of Genesis was an actual historic, worldwide (global) in its extent and effect.

- The special creation of Adam (as one man) and Eve (as one woman) and their subsequent fall into sin, is the basis for the necessity of salvation for mankind (and thus for the Gospel of Jesus Christ).

- The scientific aspects of creation are important, but are secondary in importance to the proclamation of the Gospel of Jesus Christ as Sovereign, Creator, Redeemer and Judge.

There is no better statement of the beliefs of scientific creationism than the above. Articles in *Ex Nihilo* begin with a hypothesis and end with a solution supporting Biblical scripture. Michael J. Oard is a typical example of *Ex Nihilo* authors. Oard's specialty is dinosaurs and paleontology. In a 1999 issue, Oard discusses one of the many problems that the existence of dinosaur fossils poses for creationists. He discusses a clutch of fossilized dinosaur eggs and embryos found in Argentina. The problem is that the arrangement of the fossils suggests that the dinosaurs were "…alive, laying eggs and walking around, in the midst of the catastrophic activity of that same Flood…(Oard, 1999: 3)." Oard states at the beginning of his article that there exists disagreement whether dinosaurs became extinct during or after the flood since evidence supports both theories. The author admits to belonging to the group believing that "…the dinosaur features were made early in the Flood before the waters wholly covered the earth."

Oard tells of the thousands of eggs and egg fragments recently uncovered in Patagonia, Argentina. He proposes the hypothesis these dinosaur features (creationists call fossils "features") were made during the first 150 days of the flood while some of the land was temporarily uncovered by water. Oard suggests that, during the flood, there occurred a rapid counterclockwise current that caught the dinosaurs by surprise. As a result, the Argentine dinosaurs were drowned and buried by the flood and a secondary current during the "recessive" stage of the flood eroded the sediments where the dinosaurs were first buried.

When Humans and Dinosaurs Lived Together: The Paluxy Tracks Hoax

The issue whether humans and dinosaurs lived at the same time illustrates both the scientific creationists' resistance to facts and how their theorizing falls outside established science. Scientific creationists insist humans and dinosaurs lived during the same time. They argue humans and dinosaurs co-existed in a young earth no older than ten thousand years. Since the Bible states animals were created during the first week of creation and there were no deaths before the expulsion of Adam and Eve from the Garden of Eden, it follows dinosaurs must have lived at the same time as humanity. Scientific creationists also assume that the ark included dinosaurs as part of its cargo and that some dinosaurs were alive during the post-flood era. Scientific creationists believe legends of dragons and other monsters reflect a time when dinosaurs and humans shared the world. Scientific creationist books for children typically contain images of people and dinosaurs living happily together.

Scientific creationists eagerly follow reports of sightings and rumors of living dinosaur-type animals. Scientific creationists believe the Loch Ness Monster, Bigfoot, and similar legends are examples of surviving dinosaurs and ape-like beings because the Bible mentions monsters, leviathans, and behemoths. In Job 40:15–17, a behemoth is described as: "…See its powerful loins and the muscles of its belly. Its tail is as straight as a cedar. The sinews of its thighs are tightly knit together. Its bones are tubes of bronze. Its limbs are bars of iron (New Living Tradition)." Robert T. Pennock (1999: 217) notes that the phrase "tail is as straight as a cedar" is a euphemism for male genitals rather than body size, and the description does not necessarily describe a very large animal with a tail "as long as a cedar" as the scientific creationists assume.

In a similar manner, scientific creationists are interested in sighting of creatures resembling "sea dragons" as vindication of their religious views. Since scientific creationists define the Bible as a historical document, references to monsters in both the Bible and in modern times provide support for a young earth. Mace Baker is convinced sea living dinosaurs, or sea dragons, have been sighted a number of times since the 1800s, probably something akin to ichthyosaurs (Baker, 2003: iv):

> The scriptures indicate very clearly that sea dragons were part of the original creation and are mentioned as being alive and flourishing even after the time of Noah's flood. For instance, in Psalm 74:13 we read, "Thou didst divide the

sea by thy strength: thou brakest the heads of the dragons in the waters." The Hebrew word used here for dragons is "*tannin*." This is the same Hebrew word which refers to land dragons (dinosaurs) in a variety of Scriptures including, for instance, in Malachi 1:3 which reads, "And I hated Esau, and laid his mountains and his heritage waste for the dragons of the wilderness."

Scientific creationists also insist dinosaur and human footprints exist in the same sedimentary strata since dinosaurs and humans co-existed, and insist that such combined print patterns have or will be discovered. More orthodox scientists, however, have dated the age of dinosaurs as ending roughly seventy million years before the emergence of primates. A vindication of the Young-Earth position held by scientific creationists would be the discovery of dinosaur and human footprints in the same limestone formations. Morris (1984: 332) claims a number of such tracks have been discovered since 1980, but he does not offer any references except an alleged report from a Russian newspaper.

The showcase example of simultaneous dinosaur and human tracks was reputedly unearthed near Glen Rose, Texas, near the Paluxy River where scientific creationists insist human and dinosaur tracks are mingled. As Henry M. Morris writes (Morris, 1985: 332), "…the prints are there, and they have every appearance of being authentic, showing conclusively that man and dinosaurs lived at the same time." Some footprints are bare and other sets wear sandals. A few pages after the above quote, Morris admits that some of the "human" tracks have been found to be reptilian, some sets are missing, and other are carved forgeries. A few pages later (p. 354), the caption showing a photograph of these alleged human and dinosaur tracks states, "These [tracks] are considered doubtful." However, publications from the *Institute for Creation Research* still contain references to the Paluxy tracks as proof of a young earth. Earlier, Kelly L. Segraves (1975) described the Paluxy footprints as definite proof of the falsity of evolution. Other creationists had doubts concerning the authenticity of the Paluxy tracks and traveled to Glen Rose to see whether or not the tracks were authentic and were not convinced the tracks were authentic (Numbers, 1992: 265).

Close examination by less biased investigators than Young-Earth scientific creationists shows the alleged prints at Glen Rose to have an average length of sixteen inches; one set averaged twenty-two inches long, making the weight of these humans over six hundred pounds. The spacing between tracks indicates an impossible stride of seven feet. While creationists claim these tracks were left by the giants mentioned in the Bible, the track are impossible on a human scale (Berra, 1990: 129). Experts view the tracks as having been doctored: they are without doubt forgeries or misidentified tracks of dinosaurs. Many reproductions of the supposedly human tracks have imprints of a claw on the back of each heel. Other prints upon closer investigation are dinosaur marks with sand selectively placed to make them more human-shaped. Some prints have their insteps on the outside edges rather than on the inside. Detailed investigations of enlarged prints of other tracks indicate the "human" footprints had been darkened by shellac or oil to give them more human-like contours. The tracks are actually dinosaur marks painted with a human outline (Godfrey, 1981: 25). Nevertheless, no paleoichnologists (specialists on tracks made by extinct animals) were allowed to study the tracks. Rubber impressions were made of some of the Paluxy tracks but have allegedly deteriorated beyond recognition. Copies of plaster casts of the marks cannot be obtained for additional and impartial examinations.

Additional Weaknesses of Scientific Creationism

The beliefs and statements of scientific creationism are not testable although testability is a major requirement of science. The criterion of falsibility, or testability, divides scientific information from theological, moral, and artistic statements. By contrast, scientific creationist knowledge is based on the assumption of a supernatural agency and the *manner* in which the deity created cannot be investigated, further separating scientific creationism from orthodox science. Duane Gish recognizes this point when he states (Gish, 1978: 40):

> We do not know how God created, what processes he used, *for He used processes which are not now operating anywhere in the natural universe.* This why we refer to creation as special creation. We cannot discover by scientific investigations anything about the creative processes used by the creator.

The above quote again illustrates not only the Biblical basis of the beliefs of scientific creationists but also places scientific creationists outside the scientific framework by claims that their beliefs cannot be tested and therefore cannot be disproved.

What types of explanations do scientific creationists offer that counter data supporting evolution? The explanation for the male peacock's tail display is an example of how evolutionists and creationists disagree on the interpretation of the same phenomenon. Darwinian logic says the male peacock's grand tail is used to attract mates, as are many secondary sexual characteristics found among other animals such as elk's horns and bright displays among birds (see Pennock, 1999: 199–200). Darwin found that sexual attraction was one of the major sources of natural selection: males with more visible features than other males were more likely to attract mates and therefore have more offspring.

Marion Petrie experimented with peacocks to test whether hens are in fact attracted to peacock males' displays. Petrie cut off varying numbers of tail feathers from male tail displays to test whether females were attracted differently by different numbers of tail feathers. Males with increasingly fewer "eyes" in their displays increasingly failed to attract mates (Zimmer, 2001: 237). Females accepted some loss of tail feather eyes but totally rejected those males who had less than 130 complete tail feathers rather than an average of 150.

Scientific creationist Phillip E. Johnson (1991: 31) also notes the male peacock has ornate tail feathers while the peahen is drab in comparison. He explains these gender features as "just the kind of creatures a whimsical creator might favor, but that an 'uncaring mechanical process' like natural selection would never permit to develop." Johnson is of course wrong. Natural selection has resulted in grand displays of many types and Charles Darwin wrote a book on the consequences of sexual selection in its role in evolution (*Descent of Man*). Original fieldwork, which creationists do not conduct, has shown that displays attract mates. Johnson is also willing to describe God as exhibiting a sense of humor to support his anti-evolution ideology.

Some creationists are comfortable with the notion of a god who is not only "whimsical" but also who fools people as an explanation for the variety of life and fossils. Whitcomb and Morris (1961: 345–5 and 354) suggest God may have created radioactive materials with decay products that seem to indicate an older age of the earth than the age accepted by Young-Earth creationists. That is, God created daughter elements (elements that are the result of radioactive decay) that *seem* to be the product of great age but are not. That is one reason why radioactive measures indicate an earth much older than ten thousand years. Scientific creationists argue tests to determine age using radioactive decay rates are either mistaken or the result of God's trickery. In the same way, God created stars at various distances from the galactic center to produce an illusion of billions of years as the age of the universe. This provides a varied night sky but is also a lie. Why should humans wait millions of years for distant starlight to reach the earth? God merely placed stars at different distances from the earth to give the universe an illusion of age (Morris, 1972: 61–2). If God could create Adam and Eve as adults, then logic demands God could also create a mature-seeming universe. This places God in the same category as trickster gods found in many other religious systems. Do we want to introduce into school curricula the concept of a trickster deity who created a universe that looks as if it is billions of years old but is in reality much younger? Using this logic, no evidence contradicting Biblical statements of fact can be disproved.

A more intellectually dangerous creationist belief is that sequential placing of fossils, radioactive decay, and other signs contradicting a Young-Earth theology are all tests of faith. That is, seemingly contradictory evidence placed by God is false and tests of a person's faith. This, of course, demands a blind faith that ignores all contradictory evidence. This approach to biblically contradictory evidence is difficult to answer in a logical fashion since it is impervious to empirical proof or logic. This position is similar to the one stating God lies as in the mature-earth model discussed in the first chapter, but is just as dangerous to the educational process.

The Genesis Flood

o o o o o o o o o o o o o o o o o o o o o o o o o o o o o o o o
Mature Christians, who are adequately taught in God's Word,
have no fear of historical, archaeological or scientific discoveries
which appear to nullify any portion or any statement of infallible
Scripture.

—John C. Whitcomb

The Importance of Explaining the Genesis Flood

The flood is presumed to have occurred roughly between 3000–2500 B.C. although there is no factual basis for this belief except scriptural passages. Belief in a literal worldwide flood is often a basic element in membership in Protestant fundamentalism and in scientific creationism, and separates true believers from outsiders. The Genesis flood is the central exhibit for Young-Earth scientific creationists, once called *flood geologists*, because they anchor their beliefs in a worldwide flood and its consequences. Their beliefs lose their scientific character when they cannot explain the events associated with an alleged worldwide flood. Biblical accounts of the Noachian flood contradict major elements of well-established sciences and scientific creationists must reconcile these accounts with orthodox science or lose all expectation of becoming respectable. Flood accounts conflict with central elements of geology, geophysics, meteorology, oceanography, biology, anthropology, physics, paleontology, archeology, and other disciplines. Literal acceptance of the Genesis flood and related events isolate scientific creationists from accepted scientific knowledge.

Conditions of the Pre-Flood Earth

The pre-flood earth was a more idyllic place than it is today. The land was richer in minerals and special vitamins while creatures lived longer because of their richer diet. Humans and animals were vegetarian and healthier. The antediluvian society was in a golden age (Morris, 1977a: 77), though so many persons followed Cain and sinned to a degree a worldwide destruction was necessary. This division is interpreted as an indication for the need for laws and government (Morris, 1977a: 77). If one assumes Adam and his early descendants enjoyed a lifespan of over five hundred years each and each couple had five children every one hundred years, the world's population when Adam died at the age of 930 would have been an estimated 80,000. The world's population when the flood occurred 1,656 years after the death of Adam would be 235,000,000 (Morris, 1977a: 79–80). This large number of pre-flood people is assumed by scientific creationists to have developed high-level civilizations destroyed by the flood.

Morris compared the lifespan of the Patriarchs listed in Genesis and found each generation experienced progressively shorter lives (Morris, 1977a: 85). The reasons for decreasing life spans and why pre-flood animals were larger are that Morris and other scientific creationists assert essential nutrients were washed into the oceans during and after the flood (in addition to the forces of entropy, perhaps). The richer and more abundant pre-flood food supply allowed for greater the size of animals than possible after the flood is one reason why there are no large dinosaurs today, though some may be hidden in areas where rich sediments still exist in deep lakes or ocean beds (there is no factual basis that deep lakes and ocean beds contain energy-rich material). The Bible also tells of "giants" roaming the world in the pre-flood era. Some scientific creationists feel the pre-flood conditions allowed for some humans to become giants. Other scientific creationists believe these "giants" were the offspring of women and the Sons of Satan discussed in the Jewish Bible. Scientific creationists believe there is additional support for the argument that the earth once contained more nutrients because the largest animals alive today are found in the earth's oceans. Whales and other large sea creatures take advantage of the nutrients washed from the land when it was richer, though there are no data to support this claim.

God placed a rainbow in the sky when the rains ended. The first rainbow in the history of the world showed the surviving eight humans there would never be another great flood. A rainbow at this time would have lacked impact if one had already been seen. Scientific creationists hypothesize rainbows were impossible before the flood since there were no rains or storms and the climate was "mildly warm." The constant temperature throughout the world's surface inhibited strong wind patterns thereby making storms impossible (Morris, 1977a: 77). Scientific creationists are forced to develop "just-so" stories so the events in the scriptures can be understood in a "scientific manner."

Henry M. Morris (Morris, 1998: 51–2) sums up this scientific creationist position of pre-flood weather patterns as:

> In order for the upper waters to be maintained aloft by the gases of the lower atmosphere and also to be transparent to the light of the sun, they seem to have been in the form of a vast blanket of water vapor, extending far out into space, invisible and yet exerting a profound influence on terrestrial climates and living conditions. Such a "canopy" could have caused a worldwide warm, mild climate, with only minor seasonal and latitudinal differences. This in turn would have inhibited the great air circulational patterns which characterize the present atmosphere and which constitute the basic cause of our winds, rains, and storms.
>
> There could have been no rain in the form with which we are familiar, and this is exactly the testimony of Scripture (Genesis 2:5, 6). But there was a system of rivers and seas (Genesis 1:10, 2:10–14), nourished probably by waters that had been confined under pressure beneath the lands, when the lands and the waters were separated, as well as by the low-lying vapors that were daily evaporated and recondensed (Genesis 2:6).

The quote above illustrates many of the problems faced by scientific creationists in their attempts to reconcile their religious beliefs with orthodox science. They are forced to present "just-so" stories in order to make sense of their beliefs. Morris in the quote above fabricated a novel weather system impossible under the science of physics, a "canopy," and numerous "seems," "coulds," and "probablys." The introduction of creation science materials in public schools would lead to the introduction of numerous "just-so" stories to support unique Young-Earth worldviews.

Where did the Water for the Flood Originate?

A central question concerning the flood deals with the source of enough water to flood the earth during a forty-day deluge. One creationist theory posits pre-flood land contours were flat with low, if any, mountains and no deep oceans. The ocean's water could then cover a greater extent of the land area than would be possible today. The lack of tall mountain ranges would also allow for more even global temperatures. There were no ice caps before the flood, according to scientific creationists, so they cannot be accepted as a source of floodwater.

There are two commonly accepted creationist theories that provide enough water for a worldwide flood. The first hypothesis is the existence of a canopy of water vapor mentioned above that presumably covered the world (Whitcomb,

1988: 36). This canopy would have increased the possibility of a globally comfortable weather pattern. An advantage of the water vapor theory is that it presumably kept harmful cosmic rays from reaching the surface of the earth, thereby making humans healthier and able to enjoy longer life spans. Isaiah 40:12, 22 mentions "...waters...that stretcheth out the heaven as a curtain, and spreadeth them out as a tent to dwell in (cited in Morris, 1976: 57)." Elsewhere, Morris (1977a: 25) states that this canopy helped produce a perfect earth:

> The "waters above the firmament" must have been in the form of invisible water vapor, extending far into space. They provided a marvelous "canopy" for the earth, shielding it from the deadly radiations coming from outer space and producing a wonderful "greenhouse effect," sustaining a uniformly warm, pleasant climate all around the earth. Being invisible, these water vapors were of course transparent to the light of the heavenly bodies which were to be established on the fourth day.

The water canopy might have consisted of either ice crystals or liquid water in the form of vapor. Water vapor would have been invisible for the stars would to be visible as stated in the Bible. Henry Morris (1976: 60) prefers the vapor alternative because it offers numerous explanatory advantages. These advantages in addition to those already mentioned are:

- The vapor would have increased the air pressure which in turn had positive "hyperbaric" health consequences.

- The high resulting humidity would create a lush earth vegetation with no extreme areas such as deserts or ice caps. Vegetation was needed because all pre-flood animals ate only "every green herb (Morris, 1976: 78)."

- The vapor canopy would provide dew and ground fog during the night to compensate for a lack of rain.

- The vapor provided a reservoir for the flood.

According to scientific creationists, the antediluvian vapor protected all life from harmful radiations bombarding the earth from outer space. Henry Morris (1977a: 78) states that this protection kept humans healthier because "It is known that these rays are harmful and are a chief cause of mutations and other deteriorative activity in living flesh." Morris offers no references to support this implausible statement, though unsupported declarations that seem authoritative are common in the literature of scientific creationism. Gerald Aardsma also supports the canopy hypothesis to discredit radiocarbon dating. The canopy must have absorbed cosmic radiation and kept radiation from reaching living plants and animals by a factor of at least three. The low levels of radioactive carbon in fossils indicate protection by the canopy rather than great age. That is, fossils show low levels radioactive carbon because these organisms did not receive the radioactivity they would have if the water canopy had not existed (Boxer, 1987).

Geologist Aardsma also believes a canopy of water vapor existing before the flood may be impossible to prove. If the existence of the canopy is disproved, Aardsma will not reject his belief in a young earth but rather he "must be misunderstanding what's written in Genesis. I've not made the plain sense interpretation of Scripture (Boxer, 1987: 85)." Scientific creationists are immune to evidence that their position is false. If evidence is lacking, then the fault lies within their lack of understanding and not in the creationist model. Aardsma compares the Bible to a set of answers to math problems: "You can work on a problem, but it's a great consolation having the answers at the back of the book (Boxer, 1987:85)." This statement shows how little importance creationists give to empirical evidence contradicting their beliefs. This approach to knowledge is not scientific but rather religiously based. The statement also reflects the disinclination of scientific creationists to conduct original research. There is no need to do so because the "answers" are already known. The tasks for creationists are to criticize evolutionary knowledge and rationalize their beliefs.

One of the problems with the vapor canopy model is not only is there no physical evidence to support it, but the model contradicts geological and meteorological knowledge. There is only enough water on today's earth to form a thin layer of vapor encircling the earth. Another problem with the canopy model is that a vapor canopy would not be stable. Wind currents, the earth's rotation, and temperature differences among vapor, air, and land surfaces caused by day-night changes would cause precipitation in any weather system. If the vapor cover "extended far out to space," as Morris declares, the temperature gradient of the vapor would by itself cause precipitation and violent weather patterns.

The second theory of the origin of the flood's water supply is based on the Biblical passage in Genesis 1:9–10 stating a great reservoir of water was created by God under the earth during the third day of creation. This antediluvian supply of water jetted from the earth during the flood to provide enough water along with the condensing vapor canopy to engulf the world.

There remains the question of how much water was available to cover the earth, since even Mount Everest (elevation 29,000 feet) would have been covered with twenty feet of water (Ross, 1998:145) according to the Bible. A counter suggestion scientific creationists make is that Mounts Everest, Ararat, and others were created during the flood and rose as the seabed sank. In any case a world-wide flood would need four and half times the water resources existing today.

In addition, those who believe in a local flood ask why a worldwide flood was needed since most of the world was uninhabited at that time (Ross, 1998: 148). Multiple interpretations of selected Hebrew vocabulary add confusion scientific creationists ignore. To them, a literal reading of the Bible should result in only one interpretation though those believing the flood was local rather than global also claim to be literalists. The quarrel between the two groups involves the meanings of words in the original language. There are numerous examples of conflicting translations whenever the flood is discussed in Genesis. The Hebrew word *kasah* can be understood in four different ways: "covering," "residing on," "running over," and "falling upon." (Ross, 1998: 145). It can refer to a flash flood, heavy rain, or a deluge. Scientific creationists accept the last meaning since doing so implies a worldwide flood. Given this interpretation, scientific creation-ists are forced to explain where the required amount of water originated (see below).

One can also defend the occurrence of either a local or worldwide flood depending how Genesis 8:4 is interpreted. Local floodists, in contrast to scientific creationists, believe the passage in Genesis 8:4 stating that the ark landed on or near Mount Ararat actually should be interpreted differently. It would be under-standable to believe in a worldwide flood if the ark had actually landed on Mount Ararat with an elevation of almost 17,000 feet. However, according to local floodists, the scriptural passage should be translated to state the ark landed "near" rather than "on" Mount Ararat. This refers to an area in Mesopotamia that includes the mountain itself, its foothills, and more than 100,000 square miles of the Mesopotamian plain (Ross, 1998: 147). Although scientific creationists make the claim they interpret the Bible literally, there remains multiple possible mean-ings to original words.

There are also multiple possible meanings for the term *kol heharim hugebohim*, which scientific creationists define as "all the high mountains." Creationists who believe the flood was local rather than worldwide accept alternative definitions to the words above. These creationists also believe the flood must have been local because the dove that Noah sent out returned with an olive leaf. Since olive trees do not grow in high elevations, supporters of the local flood model suggest that the dove found vegetation on a low-lying hill rather than a tall mountaintop just emerging from the receding flood (Ross, 1998: 146). A year-long flood would have destroyed all vegetation and it would have taken months for an olive tree to re-establish itself, if any tree could survive being submerged for a year.

Because of these inconsistencies, scientific creationists are forced to add speculations to make their flood models plausible. Below is how Morris uses convoluted logic to explain pre-flood conditions (Morris, 1984: 281):

> Thus the antediluvian hydrologic cycle was a subterranean, earth-controlled
> cycle, unlike our present atmospheric, sun-controlled, cycle. The pressures of
> the subterranean "deep" would have to be maintained by the earth's own
> internal heat, continuously applies as it moved upward from the earth's inte-
> rior. The water leaving the great reservoirs presumably coursed through great
> natural conduits of some sort, precisely planned by their divine Creator to
> release the right amounts of warm spring waters at the intended outlets all
> over the earth. The "fountains of the deep" were "strengthened" (Prov. 8:28)
> to withstand these pressures and temperatures and thus to serve faithfully as
> long as their intended function was needed.

There is no physical evidence for any of the statements in the above quote
because Morris has woven plausible, non-empirical rationales for selected Biblical
passages. The above statements make sense only if readers are willing to ignore all
recognized geological evidence. These kinds of elaborations based on Biblical
scripture rather than on empirical evidence belong in comparative religion rather
than in science classes.

There is the question of what happened to the large amount of water needed
to cause a worldwide flood. Hugh Ross (Ross, 1998: 148) suggests the floodwa-
ters receded back to their original underground locations. This claim posits the
existence of large reservoirs, or aquifers, under the earth that have not yet been
discovered. Scientific creationists need to prove the existence of these reservoirs if
this claim is ever to be believed.

They are aware of the many problems posed by the need to account for the
origin and the amount of water needed to cover the earth. John Woodmorappe
(2000) acknowledges that accepted meteorological processes do not account for a
forty-day rainfall that could cover the earth. His answer to this problem is typical
of the work by scientific creationists. Woodmorappe suggests that localized
super-hurricanes could have provided the force needed to lift underground superheated water into the atmosphere.

Woodmorappe proposes that super-hurricanes, or hypercanes, would have the
strength to throw vast amounts of underground water into the atmosphere. Only
large volcanoes could have formed these hypothetical hypercanes. These volcanoes heated large volumes of oceanic water to scalding temperatures to form conditions encouraging large hurricanes, or hypercanes, though there is no evidence

offered that there exist traces of volcanoes large enough to form the imagined hypercanes. The resulting temperature differences between the superheated water and the atmosphere could, to Woodmorappe's satisfaction, form large typhoons or hypercanes (Woodmorappe, 2000: 124–5):

> If the air-currents aloft are favorably positioned, the rising moisture-bearing air will be driven into a pattern that starts to circulate.

An advantage of this hypothesis, aside from explaining how underground waters were raised into the atmosphere to provide forty days and nights of rain at an estimated rate of one-half inch per hour, is that the alleged hypercanes are so powerful only a limited number is needed for the desired effects. The hypercanes ceased when (Woodmorappe, 2000: 126):

> ...the tectonic processes during the Flood caused large waves to develop. These snuffed out the hypercanes. Thus we had only 40 days of rainfall, instead of rainfall through the year-long flood. Most of the water which flooded the continents came from the oceans as they increased in depth, and not from the hypercane-induced precipitation.

Woodmorappe presented a series of plausible ad hoc hypotheses or "just-so" stories by inventing a concept having no theoretical or empirical validity. He argues that it might have been possible for underground water to be raised into the atmosphere and condense into rain as it cooled if one also assumes volcanoes large enough to provide the heat needed. Woodmorappe admits this lack of reliable information as he concludes his article by saying (Woodmorappe, 2000: 127):

> Hypercanes *may* well turn out to be the 'missing link' between oceanic waters and global rainfall during the global Flood. Creationists with a background in the atmospheric sciences need to conduct further research on hypercanes. *If* such research validates the hypercane concept, and answers the lingering questions about dissipative heating, we will be much closer to understanding how the 40 days and 40 nights of rainfall took place during the early stages of the Biblical Flood (Genesis 7:4, 12) [emphasis added].

In the above quote, Woodmorappe assumes hypercanes exist, though they are the result of his imagination. There is, however, no evidence that hypercanes ever or could have ever existed. As we pointed out earlier, scientific creationists know the answers and seek to "explain" their hypotheses in order to appear scientific. While other creationists are willing to depend on miracles to explain their positions, scientific creationists are forced to invent pseudo-scientific concepts. These conclusions hint at the amount of faith needed to maintain scientific creationist arguments in the face of a total lack of empirical support for their assumptions and conclusions.

Additional Problems Concerning the Flood and Its aftermath

The flood creates other problems for scientific creationists. For example, it is difficult to account for a rapid increase in population after the destruction of virtually all humanity, animals, and vegetation not in the ark. Nevertheless, the human population had increased enough in a few hundred years to provide the labor to build the Tower of Babel and, after its destruction, to separate into tribes. Henry Morris (1984: 430) states that there were seventy families when the Tower was built. These are said to be the origins of the seventy major language groups in the world today.

Morris believes the failure to complete the Tower of Babel was accompanied by not only the emergence of mutually unintelligible languages, but with also the introduction of "false" doctrines known today (Morris, 1984: 109):

> The real author of this vast religious complex—this great world religion of pantheistic, polytheistic, demonist, astrological, occultistic, humanistic evolutionism—can be none other than the one who is called in the Bible as the "god of this world…"

Segraves (1975) additionally interprets Genesis 6:11 as evidence that fallen angels encouraged (and participated in) "corrupt" behavior among humans, thereby angering God and causing the flood. These Satanic practices forced God to destroy all land dwellers except Noah, his immediate family, and selected land dwellers (Segraves, 1975: 129):

> The remaining verses of Genesis 6 give strong evidence to support the concept that fallen angels participated in depraved acts with people in the days before the Flood. We are told in verse 11 that *all* flesh was corrupt. So horrid were these acts, so Satanic in their nature, that is was necessary for God to totally destroy the world with water, condemning some angels to an existence in chains as a warning for the futures. There is strong evidence to support this

concept that the whole world was totally destroyed with water in the not-so-distant past. Such a destruction lends credence to the reality of the Word of God in the life of the Christian and certainly acts as strong warning of judgment to those who refuse to accept the Biblical record.

Segraves is typical of Young-Earth creationists in giving the flood the center stage of his speculations. Segraves also finds numerous passages in the Bible clearly stating to him that fallen angels caused humanity's fall and a need for the Noachian flood. Moreover, Segraves understands some Biblical passages state that these fallen angels—Satan's minions—remain active today. He believes that fallen angels pilot Unidentified Flying Objects (UFOs) (Segraves, 1975: 164):

> The Satanic entities posing as angels and ministers of light are deceiving people in these last days. In an attempt to destroy the pure and life-giving message of the Bible they have come as visitors from outer space. But please remember, there is no scientific, empirical evidence for the existence of any being living outside our solar system.

Segraves' Biblical interpretations of UFO sightings are probably just as logical as anyone else's. It is nevertheless a short logical step to believe that the flood was forced onto God by fallen angels who continue to tempt humanity to sin. The acceptance of these "saucerians" by Segraves is just one example of the dangers of introducing creationist thought into the classroom. Scientific creationists find that the Bible gives "strong evidence" to support a large variety of theories about nature and the world in general. However, the basis of these beliefs is religious rather than scientific.

Another concern of creationists related to explaining the flood is the deposits of coal and petroleum under the earth's surface. Orthodox scientists say these deposits are the remains of organic matter that have been under great pressure for millions of years. Young-Earth scientific creationists cannot accept this view. They are forced by their own theology to explain the existence of coal and petroleum as the result of tectonic pressures during the flood. Scientific creationists have searched in vain for evidence that coal and petroleum were formed roughly four thousand years ago.

One strategy used to explain Young-Earth petroleum deposits is to claim that million of years are not required for the formation of oil deposits. Kelly L. Segraves (1975: 144) summarized this conventional Young-Earth creationist position clearly:

The formation of coal and oil does not require millions of years, as the evolutionists sometimes claim, but can be accomplished in a relatively short period of time. Recently oil has been formed by converting a ton of garbage into a barrel of oil with the proper pressure and temperature conditions. In an hour and a half a piece of wood was converted to coal in Germany by using a pile driver. This was not their intention, but they applied the right amount of pressure and converted the material into coal. The proper amount of pressure determines the formation of coal and oil, not long periods of time.

George McCready Price first proposed in 1935 that coal and petroleum deposits were formed either four thousand years ago or more recently. He hoped scientific creationist petroleum geology would prove a better guide in the locating new oil fields than orthodox methods, though no petroleum fields have been located by creationist methodologies. Scientific creationists are currently searching Mount St. Helens for evidence of recent coal formation. Hundreds of trees were washed into a lake when St. Helens erupted in 1980. Creationist geologist Steve Austin expects this layer of wood on the lake's bottom to form into coal within a few years (Boxer, 1987). Austin is also trying to show that the Noachian flood formed petrified wood in a short amount of time similar to oil, gas, and coal deposits.

There is also the question how so much coal and petroleum could be produced within two thousand years or during a forty-day flood. Orthodox scientists have established that the earth's land surface could not have produced enough biomass to form all existing fossil fuels in one short period of time. To answer this criticism, two scientific creationists proposed that floating forests on the earth's seas could have added to the mass of vegetation needed for the conversion into fossil fuels. These vegetation mats were destroyed during the flood (Schönknecht and Scherer, 1997: 280) and sank to the bottom of the oceans and "were subjected to pressure condition which led to a rapid formation of coal." These authors conclude (p. 281):

> According to the calculations above, there would have been enough space on the Earth's surface during the pre-Flood period for some of the vegetation in today's lignite deposits to have grown…On the other hand, it is also possible that an unknown portion of Tertiary lignites was formed during the post-Flood mega-successions, the vegetation thus being buried by catastrophes subsequent to the Flood.

Critics would expect these floating forests to have re-emerged after the flood, but there is no evidence of their existence. Since land-based forests managed to re-establish themselves after the flood, empirical proof is needed to show that floating forests also existed but could not re-establish themselves on the post-flood oceans.

Problems With Fossils

The presence of large coal and petroleum deposits is not the only datum creationists cannot explain easily. There is also the question of the large number of fossils that have been discovered. Scientific creationists say all fossils were formed during the flood or soon after the post-flood cataclysms. Paleontologist Robert E. Sloan has been studying the fossils in the Karoo Formation. He estimates that there may be 800 billion animals, most of them the size of a fox, fossilized in the Formation. If this estimate is valid, then there would have been at least 2,100 animals per acre when the flood began (Schadewald, 1982: 13). The large number of fossils raises the question how so many animals could have found enough to eat in a very crowded earth. A more convincing argument is that these animals lived over a span of millions of years rather than two thousand years.

Scientific creationists state simple organisms died quickly during the flood and were deposited on the bottom layers. Larger animals were able to climb to higher ground before they drowned as the waters rose. Scientific creationists cannot explain why flying reptiles are not found in the same strata as modern birds. Whitcomb and Morris (1961: 276) state that the seeming—but misleading—sequential drowning caused the arrangements of fossils in one stratum or another. Smaller animals could not travel to higher ground as fast as large animals and were thus drowned by the rising flood first. Other animals may have been both too slow and stupid to seek higher ground. These statements are nonsensical since not all larger animals are faster or less alert than smaller ones. In addition, fossils of larger megafauna are located in strata lower than their smaller descendants, reversing the order predicted by scientific creationists.

Land animals, for example, do not appear below the Paleozoic strata because, according to scientific creationists, that was when "the smaller and less agile of the amphibians and reptiles were overtaken and swept into the Deluge sediments." Why were no dinosaurs caught on the higher grounds along with modern horses and humans? There is evidence large numbers of small dinosaurs existed which were faster and more nimble than humans and many contemporary animals. Yet no fossils of these animals are found in the same strata with human remains. In addition, large dead animals float, and it seems logical to expect that some dinosaurs would have floated to higher elevations before being buried in mud. Yet no younger sedimentary strata include such fossils (Bowler, 1984: 345).

There is another unanswered problem dealing with the flood. Creationists claim the flood and accompanying upheavals mixed up dead bodies. Any seeming sequence of dead bodies and fossils in various rock layers are misunderstood because scientific creationists say no sequence exists. In response to this claim, fossilized plants are rigidly layered by type. Plants are divided into two types. The older type—non-flowering gymnosperms—use winds to pollinate, as do today's ferns. Modern flowers, angiosperms, have more complex sexual parts and flowers as part of their reproductive system. There are no flowering plants located below sedimentary strata containing the earliest gymnosperms fossils. One would have expected fossilized gymnosperms and angiosperms to be found together if all plants were created at the same time and were mixed together during the flood. Yet fossil beds show only gymnosperms in strata deposited millions of years before angiosperms emerged (Godfrey, 1983: 203). Orthodox science does much better in predicting and explaining phenomena than does scientific creationism.

Scientific creationists also claim that hydrodynamic sorting created other fossil layers, including those containing animals. Yet no skeletons of modern horses have been found in the sedimentary layers where earlier forms of horses are located because existing fossil layers are too uniform to have been formed during Noah's flood. These fossil sequences began the search for a better understanding of animal life during the eighteenth century when fossils began to be analyzed by scientists. Young-Earth creationists have not been able to explain these sequences contradicting their theology.

Scientific creationists explain the existence of layers of fossils by suggesting that there must have been a number of lesser floods. Ken Ham states (1993: 12):

> By the way, the Flood of Noah's day probably occurred just over 4,500 year ago. Creationists believe that this even formed many of the fossil layers around the Earth. (Additional fossil layers were formed by other floods as the Earth settled down after the great Flood.) Thus, the dinosaur fossils which were formed as a result of this Flood were probably formed about 4,500 years ago, *not* millions of years ago.

The reasoning above, as usually unsupported by any evidence, does not explain why certain fossils are found together and why various forms of animals are consistently found in the same strata. Scientific creationists add explanations upon explanations to make their religious beliefs match physical evidence. This necessitates making increasingly complicated "just-so" stories.

Finally, the accompanying extreme volcanic activity would have produced large amounts of dust, ashes, and debris that would have changed the earth's weather patterns for decades. It would have been difficult for vegetation to re-establish itself quickly under those conditions and food for humans and animals would have been scarce for years if not longer. Certainly, there would have been no living olive trees to provide an olive branch for a dove to bring back to the ark as a sign to Noah that the flood was over and the waters receding.

We have seen a belief in a worldwide flood conflicts with well-established information found in scientific disciplines dealing with the formation of the earth, climate patterns, botany, geology, and others. There are additional problems dealing with issues related to the scientific creationist insistence that a literal worldwide flood occurred. These issues are discussed in the next chapter within the context of the events presumably taking place within the ark while it floated during the flood and those events taking place after the flood receded.

Noah's Ark

o o o o o o o o o o o o o o o o o o o o o o o o o o o o o o o o o o
Many people have gone to Mt. Ararat to try to find Noah's Ark.
I have been there more than ten times.

—*John D. Morris*

The Importance of the Ark to Scientific Creationists

The significance of Noah's ark is more central to scientific creationists than the Shroud of Turin to Roman Catholics. Before the Shroud was shown to be a forgery, Catholics felt it represented concrete proof of Christ's existence and resurrection. Similarly, scientific creationists see locating and producing evidence of the ark as concrete vindication of their belief in the literal truth of Biblical text, especially in terms of showing proof of an actual global flood. Such views have encouraged more than forty expeditions since 1945 to search for the ark. All have proven fruitless though hearsay tells of persons talking to those who claim to have seen the ark. Some creationists believe God does not want the ark found until a later age and is keeping it hidden through supernatural intervention. Because creationists seldom conduct field studies or engage in original research, the large number of attempts to locate the ark reflects the ark's importance.

Tradition holds the ark landed on or near Mount Ararat in Turkey. Kent E. Hovind (n.d.) believes the ark is located seventeen miles from Mount Ararat but within the "Mountains of Ararat" area as described in the Bible. Henry Morris (1984: 254) believes the ark can be found at the center of the earth that is located slightly west of Mt. Ararat, north of Jerusalem, and northeast of the site where the tower of Babel was located. The central location of the ark's landing made it ideal for repopulating the earth. In addition, Morris claims from his analysis of Biblical passages that the city of Jerusalem is also located near the computer-determined geographic center of the earth as the ideal site "for evangelizing and ruling the earth." Morris does not explain how a computer program located the center of the earth's surface at that precise location. If a central location were needed, it would have been better to consider a more accessible location to land and water travel.

Construction and Materials of the Ark

The dimensions of the ark are explicitly described in Genesis 6:15. Noah was told to build an ark three hundred cubits long, fifty cubits wide, and thirty cubits tall. The actual size of a cubit is uncertain. The Hebrews used two measures they called a cubit: a long or royal cubit (20.4 inches) and a common cubit (17.5 inches). Scientific creationists commonly use the shorter cubit, making the dimensions of the ark 438 feet long, 73 feet wide, and 34 feet high (Whitcomb and Morris, 1961: 10). The length of the ark would be almost the same as a World War II escort aircraft carrier. The ark displaced an estimated 19,940 tons of water, making it the largest vessel built until 1884. If the longer cubit measure is used, the ark would be larger and more improbable.

Scientific creationists determined the ark had a carrying capacity of 522 railroad cars. This volume is said to be large enough to accommodate all the land animals needed to be loaded on the ark (Morris, 1985: 253) with enough space left over for supplies and the living quarters for eight humans. K. L. Segraves (1975: 133) believes the ark below the deck was divided into three levels. The first floor was given over to animals known today; the second contained Noah and family members; the third and lowest floor contained recreation areas and space for species that became extinct during and after the flood. The top deck was presumably the roof of the ark.

The ark was made of gopher wood according to the King James Version of the Bible, though there is no such wood known today and its specific qualities are unknown. Some creationists believe the gopher wood was laminated with pitch, much like plywood is made today. If so, the ark is presumed to have been stronger than modern steel ships (Ham and Dinsmore, 1997: 13). Ham and Dinsmore note the original word "gopher" is similar to the Hebrew "kaphar" which is translated as "atonement." This means to them the ark was divinely protected "within and without" (Genesis 6:14) by God and as a result the ark did not need to be well constructed according to recognized modern construction principles. Ham and Dinsmore support the view that God personally protected the ark during its voyage, and they also believe the ark's door "was closed...by the hand of God..." after the animals had been in the ark for seven days (Ham and Dinsmore, 1997: 3). Not all literal creationists accept the hypothesis that the ark was miraculously protected by God and therefore did not have to be well built. Scientific creationists discuss the ark within more "scientific" parameters and avoid including miraculous intervention as much as possible.

A problem exists when reconciling the scientific creationists' explanation of the material used to make the ark waterproof. Scientific creationists claim that coal and petroleum were formed during and after the flood (Whitcomb and Morris, 1961: 277–8 and 434–6). However, pitch is a hydrocarbon similar to petroleum (Moore, 1983: 4), and there should have been none available while the ark was being built. Henry Morris refuses to accept the word "pitch" in a literal fashion to avoid this seeming contradiction and suggests the term probably refers to a material not yet determined.

Scientific creationists interpret the size of the ark as indicating the flood was global rather than local since the ark had to be large enough to store all representative kinds of animals and provender for one year. Scientific creationists also point out animals would have been able to escape to higher ground if the flood had been local and an ark would not have been needed (Morris, 1985: 253). The size of the ark, however, creates problems for the more skeptical. The practical length for wooden ships without metal supports is 300 feet. Wooden ships longer than 300 feet warp and twist under sail and the hulls are no longer watertight (Tiffin, 1994: 85). Ships longer than 300 feet can only be effective if constructed of metal. The longest six-mast wooden ship was the *U.S.S. Wyoming* built during the early part of the nineteenth century. The length of the *Wyoming* was 329 feet; it could only be sailed near the coast because it leaked and was unsafe under rough seas.

Although Morris and others claim experiments with models show the ark would be stable under storm conditions, there are no published accounts (Tiffin, 1994: 86) that a rectangular object would be seaworthy under extreme conditions. A ship the size and shape of the ark could not float safely in rough seas for one year. It is also doubtful the ark could have survived the extremely large storms presumably taking place during the flood. According to scientific creationists, it was at this time the mile-deep Grand Canyon was made and the continents separated from each other at great speeds. There also must have been tsunamis throughout the global ocean because of the unprecedented amounts of water released from the skies and from under the ground. There were also extensive volcanic upheavals, and the raising and lowering of landmasses must have created large waves. Scientific creationists also say the waters covered all land with a minimum depth of fifteen cubits. Since the ark's draft was also fifteen cubits

(Whitcomb and Morris, 1961: 2), currents, wave troughs, and tides endangered the ark when it passed over emerging mountains.

The construction of the ark took one hundred and twenty years (Ham and Dinsmore, 1997: 16; Whitcomb, 1988: 24). Creationists do not explain how the ark's wood did not rot during this construction period though there is always the possibility of a supernatural intervention as an explanation or that gopher wood had qualities not found in today's wood. Scientific creationists also assume people were stronger and wiser before the flood and that they were capable of construction feats as good or better than those found today (Ross, 1998: 117). R. G. Elmendorf notes that Noah was over five hundred years old when he built the ark and therefore had the time to invent construction and building techniques unknown today. Elmendorf (1983: 39) also reminds us that people before the flood were more intelligent and Noah could have invented whatever he needed to construct the ark. As Ken Ham (2003: 1) states:

> The bible doesn't record much information about the world before the Flood, but the people of this time were very intelligent. Some began to build highly developed cities. The Bible records that some people lived to be almost a thousand years old. Think about what you could learn and accomplish if you could live several hundred years.

In addition, Elmendorf feels Noah could easily have used metal braces, metal fasteners, and the like. There is, however, no archeological evidence that metalworking existed in Turkey four thousand years ago. He also extrapolates from relevant Biblical passages to mean that the Bible does not state that *only* gopher wood was used. It is feasible to Elmendorf that other woods and metals could have been used *in addition* to gopher wood. Elmendorf also assumes that gopher wood probably swelled when wet to seal the ark from leaking. Finally, Elmendorf states he could build a full-sized replica of the ark with only himself and four assistants. It is questionable whether such a ship could survive the great storms, "fountains of the great deep," and the undersea volcanoes that took place during the flood. Scientific creationists have not yet built a functional replica of the ark to sail on the seas.

Other scientific creationists have speculated on methods used in the construction of the ark. Ham and Dinsmore (1997: 17) assume that Noah "could have easily used high speed circular saws and other labor saving, precision tools in the process of building the Ark." Other creationists feel Noah could have hired laborers and sub-contractors to help build the ark and to provide supplies. In addition, Noah had superior draft animals unavailable today because Noah and his sons could have enlisted dinosaurs to help with construction (Ham and Dinsmore, 1997: 18):

> Can you imagine what a triceratops could do, with its giant tusks and protective bony crest over its head? Attributes of that animal can remind one of the diesel-powered, hydraulic lumber-handling machines of today. Were we able to look back in time, it would be no surprise to discover that God designed many great creatures, including some of the dinosaurs, to help man with construction projects.

Creationist books for children continue to show not only dinosaurs in the ark, but also mastodon-like animals carrying lumber to the ark's construction site (Dooley, 2003). Noah did not build a rudder or masts for the ark and contemporary images of the ark show a closed, rectangular box with no sails or rudder. Hovind suggests a rudder and masts were not needed since the ark was not built to go in any specific direction. It was to float in random directions until the waters had receded. Other creationists believe God must have protected the ark from tidal waves, etc. and directed it to land on Mount Ararat or in the surrounding area.

The large size of the ark raises other questions. The seemingly excess capacity of the ark concerns some scientific creationists since the ark was only one-third full during its voyage. Why was Noah told to build a much larger ark than necessary? Doing so indicates lack of planning and faulty design on the part of God. Kelly L. Segraves, who also believes UFOs are piloted by fallen angels, proposes that one deck was reserved (Segraves, 1975: 133):

> ...for the bowling alley, badminton area, shuffleboard, and swimming pool. Or perhaps that space was used for animals which became extinct before out [sic] time.

The question still remains why the ark's dimensions were so large. One proposition is that the excess capacity of the ark was for anyone who might have heeded Noah's warning to enter the ark but did not. Since God Himself dictated the ark's dimensions, the reason for its large size remains a mystery.

The Animals in the Ark

There is the question of how the animals traveled to the ark's location. Some scientific creationists believe all of the types of animals lived in the general area where the ark was built. Representatives of all species could have lived in the same area because the world's climate before the flood was the same.

How did the animals enter the ark? Genesis 7 describes the animals entering the ark the same day the rains and flooding began. Whitcomb and Morris (1961) estimate that 30,000 or so larger animals and millions of insects entered the ark. How did 30,000 large animals manage to enter through the ark's only door in one day (John Woodmorappe estimates 16,000 animals)? How did slugs, caterpillars, koalas, and sloth avoided being crushed since larger animals had only two seconds each to enter the ark and find their places. Meanwhile, millions of insects were also flying and crawling into the ark. Ken Ham (1999: 28) and other scientific creationists assume God miraculously brought the animals to and into the ark because otherwise the process would have been impossible.

We have seen that antediluvian earth had no local or severe weather patterns and there were no rains before the flood. All animals, according to Morris (2000: 36), were able to live anywhere they wished because of earth's uniform, comfortable climate. Representatives of each type of animals did not have to travel long distances to reach the ark. Whitcomb and Morris (1961) deal with issues related to how animals reached the ark. First, they suggest that no one knows where the ark was built; no one knows which animals had to travel, if they did at all. Second, no one knows the global distribution of animals before the flood. Australian marsupials may have been distributed throughout the pre-flood earth. Third, slow moving animals could have reached the ark no matter where they were since the construction of the ark took 120 years, even if we assume the migration of local animals (if there were any local ecological niches) and that animals did not begin their migrations earlier than 120 years before the flood. Fourth, it is wrong for critics to assume the same pair of animal reached the ark and the migration to the ark could have taken many generations.

Once in the ark, the animals were first fed and then began their hibernation (Morris, 2000: 37):

> Most or all of the animals had been created with genetic potential for both migration and hibernation if and when weather conditions should warrant, and these had evidently been directed by their Creator first to migrate to the ark and then to relax into a state of hibernation as the sky began to darken and the temperature to fall as the flood was about to break on the earth.

The number of animals in the ark remains a matter of discussion among scientific creationists. Genesis reads that representatives of *all* land animals were to enter the ark. Creationists assume that not all species were necessary, because the

Bible says that "all types" were to be saved. Whitcomb and Morris feel that "type" means "families" rather than species, though this is speculation on their part rather than Biblical. Thus, one type of feline or canine would be enough to preserve the type. Two dogs, for example, would be enough to parent all species of canines and eight generic dogs were the ancestors of the wolf, coyote, domestic dog, and all other canines (Morris, 1984: 378; Hovind, n.d.). There is some confusion exactly how many animals entered the ark. Was one pair of elephants enough to represent all species? Mammoths were perhaps too large to enter the ark and were left outside to drown as one creationist suggested. The existence of mammoths is an enigma because they had long hair to protect themselves from low temperatures though scientific creationists insist the pre-flood earth had a mild climate and no cold areas as yet existed.

Genetic theory suggests one or three pairs representing all canines would not allow for an adequate genetic pool. Inbreeding due to limited gene variations causes multiple defects, including infertility. The belief that one pair, or possibly eight animals (scientific creationists differ as to how many of one type of "good" animals entered the ark), was the ancestor of a viable species runs counter to genetic knowledge. Further, the development of sub-types from dog to wolf, coyote, etc. suggests the process would be the result of evolutionary mechanisms unless one posits miracles taking place. Although scientific creationists attempt to explain their beliefs using a naturalistic framework, the "science" in their title quickly breaks down and the need for explanations using a supernatural agent quickly emerges.

Creationists claim that only a small proportion of animals are larger than sheep, including dinosaurs. Adolescents of larger animals rather than adults could also have entered the ark to further reduce the storage space needed. Less space would also have been needed if animals hibernated during all or part of the year long voyage. The issue of the need for space for the animals in the ark to exercise is not discussed.

The animals are said to have hibernated during part of their stay in the ark. Scientific creationists assume that at least some had to be fed. Since animals were vegetarian before the flood, the ark needed to carry hay for most animals. Scientific creationists also do not explain how special diets, such as nectar and fruit, were provided. Many animals such as penguins, praying mantises, and bats now eat only living foods and what they ate before they became carnivores remains unexplained (Moore, 1983: 28). A pair of lions would require roughly seventy pounds of fresh meat a day if they ate meat at this time. There is also the problem of storing large amounts of fresh meat before refrigeration had been invented. A pair of elephants would need roughly 160 metric tons of hay during the year's voyage (McGowan, 1984: 56). Since Henry Morris would define elephants as useful to humans, the ark would have had to store 1,280 metric tons of hay in the ark just for the elephants. Scientific creationists have not yet dealt convincingly with this issue how animals were fed while on the ark and afterwards. The assumption of hibernation solves many problems.

In addition to feeding the ark's animals, there is the question of the disposal of the manure excreted by thirty thousand or more animals. Whitcomb (1988: 32) assumes animals did not excrete during the year, thus solving the problem of the amount of labor needed to keep cages, nests, etc clean. Other creationists have hazarded guesses how the animals were fed and how waste material was handled (see below).

Robert A. Moore (1983: 32) conducted a survey of the over one hundred zoos listed in the 1980 *International Zoo Yearbook*. These zoos had an average of one staff to twenty-five animals and the ark would have needed at least one thousand caregivers if one assumes the ark carried 30,000 animals, ignoring the millions of insects on board. Even if most animals hibernated for some time, the estimated number of animals eight adults tended would have to been too great a responsibility unless divine intervention is part of the answer.

The ark's crew had to take care of the ark itself in addition to themselves and animals. Even well built smaller ships take in water that must be pumped out while larger ships are impossible to keep afloat unless machines continuously pump out seepage. These and other chores would have kept Noah and the others very busy during a year of the worst climatic and geological changes ever experienced.

Scientific creationists have not yet solved the problem of how enough water was stored and kept fresh for almost a year. Creationists assume it rained only for forty days, so there was over three hundred days when no rain could be collected. There is also the question whether the rainwater could have been drunk if it had been brought up from underground storage by volcanic irruptions. The seawater would have been salty, full of silt and minerals, contained dead bodies, and therefore unhealthy for animals to drink.

John Woodmorappe authored a remarkable 306 pages document defending the credibility of the ark's containing so many animals for more than a year. Titled *Noah's Ark: A Feasibility Study* (1996), the work resembles a technical report respected land grant universities' agricultural research stations publish. The report reflects scientific creationists' efforts to appear objective and, at a minimum, offers plausible, secular reasons for the acceptance of the literal existence of the ark. The abstract of the work describes the author's goal and strategy (Woodmorappe, 1996: xi):

> The work is a systematic evaluation of the housing, feeding, and waste-disposal requirements of some 16,000 animals on Noah's Ark. It is also a comprehensive rebuttal to the myriads of arguments that have been made against the Ark over the centuries. It is shown that it was possible for eight people to care for 16,000 animals, and without miraculous Divine intervention. Proven solutions are offered to the problems of animals with special diets, such as the panda and koala. The bulk of hay poses no problem, and neither do the climatic requirements of animals.

Woodmorappe's work is comprehensive in that many objections of the efficacy of the ark are presented and dismissed. While numerous (the bibliography is seventy-eight pages long) references are used, much of the work presents hypothetical solutions that are essentially "just-so" stories and "could have beens." *Noah's Ark* lacks hard data since Genesis offers little detail on the year long voyage. There is plausibility in the author's arguments comforting to Biblical literalists but no results of experiments or systematic observations are presented. The report also reflects the strategy of scientific creationists to present alleged scientific arguments. The *Institute for Creation Research* published the work while Henry M. Morris, then president of the organization, wrote the foreword. The study is representative of the scholarship scientific creationists wish to attain.

The comprehensiveness of Woodmorappe's report warrants close attention. The first "case study" in the report deals with how eight persons could have fed and taken care of nearly 16,000 animals for over a year. Woodmorappe assumes that 7,428 mammals, 4,602 birds and 3,724 reptiles were in the ark. He computes that animals occupied less than half of the total area of the ark (Woodmorappe, 1996: 16). Chapter eight is titled "Man Studies: Eight People Care for 16,000 Animals." Woodmorappe (1996: 71) claims "...eight people could definitely have taken care of tens of thousands of animals." He assumes a ten-hour workday and six-day weeks, though animals could be taken care of on the Sabbath (Luke 13:15) because the period can be defined as a crisis situation when work during the Sabbath is allowed. Another more science-oriented creationist might someday conduct an experiment in which eight persons feed 16,000 animals housed in an enclosed space for a year. This experiment would at least show the feasibility of the claim. Scientific creationists, however, show little inclination for original research or complex demonstrations. They attack and pretend to use the edifice of science but cannot add to it.

Woodmorappe assumes self-feeding devices to avoid overworking the eight humans on board. Food was also, he further assumes, stored near or overhead the animals' pens. Hay, Woodmorappe also hypothesizes, was probably compressed into pellets for ease of handling and storage. The author also assumes many specialized diets, such as the koala's dependency on fresh eucalyptus leaves, did not exist before the flood and appeared later as a consequence of micro-evolution (Woodmorappe, 1993: 117). Woodmorappe does not mention the proposition of gap creationist Walter Galusha. Galusha suggests that boa constrictors could have swallowed watermelons since all animals were vegetarian at the time. In the same manner, Woodmorappe suggests the panda's bamboo diet was caused by post-deluvian "degenerative adaptations." Animals also could have hibernated or fasted for various periods thus saving Noah the effort of feeding the animals daily. Woodmorappe (1996: 135) summarizes the efficiency of hibernation and periodical dormancy in this manner:

> Let us consider, as discussed previously, the fact that each person on the Ark cared for 2,000 animals daily. This is under the assumption of no dormancy. If now, on average, animals were dormant every other day, the number of animals to care for was halved—1,000 animals per persons per day. If dormant every two days for every one they were awake...the number dropped to 667...It is clear that long-term sleep of all or even most animals on the Ark was *not* required in order to have effect a drastic reduction in the number of animals needed to be cared for each day.

Water delivery systems can also be installed to save time and effort. Woodmorappe (1996: 76) cites a reference from the Apocrypha that pipes were used inside the ark to provide the ark with a water distribution system. Animals with specific climatic requirements were taken care in a several ways including the assumption that reptiles on the ark enjoyed greater tolerances to both temperature variations and captivity (Woodmorappe, 1996: 124–5). Woodmorappe also assumes that Noah and his family could have built environmental safeguards; he states: "For instance, concave mirrors could have been used to concentrate sunlight into certain areas of the Ark...To effect a temperature gradient, for example, elongated reptile-bearing cages could have had one end bathing in heat and the other end in cold." There no suggestion in Genesis that this had been done; the whole discussion is made up of ad hoc propositions or "just-so" stories. We have previously noted the many "seems" and "coulds" used by scientific creationists instead of valid evidence.

Attempts like Woodmorappe's to answer practical questions raised by the story of Noah are based on speculation rather than empirical evidence. Some of the statements, such as the numbers of people required to care for 16,000 animals or more—the numbers vary according to author—are open to testing never been conducted. When faced with evidence that challenges a strict interpretation of the Noachian legend, scientific creationists rely on divine intervention to reverse or modify the operation of the natural world as we now understand it. The introduction of this type of explanation into school curricula as co-equal with scientific methods of inquiry and standards of proof would undermine the educational process.

Scientific creationist John C. Whitcomb (1988:33–4) believes the animals on the ark hibernated and their bodily functions were at a minimum, thus making the care of animals easier. Whitcomb responds to critics that Genesis 6:21 ("And take thou unto thee of all food that is eaten, and thou shalt gather *it* to thee; and it shall be for food for thee, and for them.") states plainly animals on the ark did not need to eat during their year long voyage. Whitcomb (1988: 34) interprets the passage as meaning that the stored food supply was not for daily feedings but only for the first week after entering the ark. Whitcomb thinks that some of the animals might have been tired from their journey to the ark and would have needed immediate nourishment. These animals gorged themselves on the food Noah provided and then God placed them into a state of hibernation. There is no Biblical reference supporting such allegations and this interpretation differs from those made by other scientific creationists. Whitcomb further states (Whitcomb, 1988: 29) the ark was so comfortable and safe that the animals would have accepted the humans on the ark as their protectors and friends. Whitcomb also interprets the fact animals stayed in the ark for seven days before the flooding began as time spent allowing the animals to become accustomed to their pens.

Whitcomb (1988: 34) writes the number of animals in the ark remained constant during their year's confinement. A year in enclosed cages could have resulted in numerous pregnancies and overcrowding of short-lived but prolific pairs of organisms such as insects, shrews, rabbits, etc., but Whitcomb (1988: 34) assumes no pregnant females entered the ark and none conceived during their stay in the ark. Scientific creationists have not explained how insects living less than a year avoided extinction if they could not propagate. Moreover, did cicadas enter the ark as nymphs? Adult cicadas live only a week or so while nymphs live underground for seventeen years.

In addition, these animals would need energy soon after becoming fully awake. Noah and the other surviving adults would have had to feed all animals for a period of time while the waters receded and plant life was re-established. These animals could not have found vegetable matter to eat for at least several months. The land had been flooded and scoured by waves, rising and falling continents, and extensive volcanic action. It would have demanded months for new vegetation to mature enough to provide both seeds for the next season and to feed a large number of animals. Although most scientific creationists are ambiguous on this point, many (Oard, 2003) believe an ice age occurred soon after the flood and the land would not have been able to support a growing season. Scientific creationists are also vague as to when some animals became carnivores.

Dispersion of the Ark's Animals and their Survival after the Flood

How did animals reach their present locations after their departure from the ark? For example, marsupial mammals but no placental mammals are found in Australia. Diluviologist John Woodmorappe (1999: 7–11) states the interior regions of the new continents were cold because volcanic upheavals taking place during the flood released dust that blocked the sun. This is how creationists explain the evidence of ice ages geologists have discovered throughout the world. Only the seacoasts were warm enough to sustain life. Animals left the ark and followed these warm bands of exposed land to their final destinations, causing, according to Woodmorappe, "very different animals to end upon different continents." In addition some animals may have been taken to various parts of the world by their human owners (Woodmorappe, 1999: 3):

> The postdiluvian peoples, after their post-Babel dispersion, probably introduced different animals to different continents (such as Australian marsupials, South American mammals, and Madagascaran primates)…South America, Australia, and the islands of Madagascar are all in direct line of maritime routes emanating from the Middle East, and hence are natural stopping points for the postdiluvian peoples.

How did marsupials travel from Mount Ararat to Australia? Many marsupials do not travel well, nor move very quickly. J. C. Whitcomb (1973) believes they moved from Turkey to Australia using a land bridge that must have once connected Asia and Australia. In a later book, Whitcomb succinctly explains how kangaroos both reached the ark and migrated to Australia (Whitcomb, 1988: 26):

Question: How could kangaroos have traveled from Australia to Noah's Ark? *Answer:* at least two each of all the kinds of air-breathing animals—including kangaroos— must have lived on the same continent where the Ark was built, so they could come to Noah by divine guidance (Gen. 6:20; 7:9) without having to cross oceans.

Question: How did kangaroos reach Australia from Mount Ararat after the flood? *Answer:* A great land bridge apparently connected Asia and Australia in the early post-Flood period. During this most intense phase of the "ice age," such vast quantities of water were locked in the polar regions that ocean levels were hundreds of feet lower than they are now. The National Geographic *Atlas of The World* (1981) clearly shows the shallow continental shelf that extends even now from Indochina almost to Australia.

There is no evidence of such a land bridge but creationists must assume similar mechanisms to allow migration to places where only certain animals live. Further, marsupials must have traveled quickly to avoid carnivores. Marsupials were fortunate they were able to reach Australia just after the land bridge sank into the seas but before carnivores reached Australia to protect from placental mammals.

An expert in diluviology, John Woodmorappe is more specific concerning the migration of marsupials to Australia, though his theory contradicts John Whitcomb's earlier statements on the topic. Woodmorappe believes both theories that animals dispersed by themselves after leaving the ark and that humans took specific sets of animals with them after the destruction of the Tower of Babel. Woodmorappe (1999: 10) states:

> It would have been no great difficulty for a post-Babel adventurer to have brought with him seventeen pairs of marsupial kinds from the Middle East to Australia. Having a reminder of one's homeland is a powerful motivator for the introduction of animals...and, if some of the descendants of Noah's family had grown accustomed to marsupials near their respective homes in the Middle East area [near Mount Ararat], they would thus have the motivation to take marsupials with them.

The above scenario sounds plausible although there is no reliable proof it occurred. There is no fossil evidence for such migration patterns or geological evidence of recently sunk land bridges Woodmorappe claims existed four thousand years ago. It would have been more plausible for this "adventurer" to have also brought with him more useful animals such as camels, dogs, and horses. They would also have been very helpful during the long journey from Turkey to Australia. Why would this pioneer take *all* of the Australian marsupials? If he had "grown accustomed" to them, it is reasonable to assume others had also grown to like the marsupials and insisted some remain with them. Why would Noah's family members become "accustomed" to marsupial moles and wombats? These live in burrows, are sedentary, and would not make good pets or companions. Evolutionary and geological theories provide better explanations why marsupials are found in a limited part of the earth.

We can also assume that some of the animals would have died along the journey and left their remains to be discovered during modern times. In addition, most animals have restricted diets are not found throughout the world and it would have been difficult for animals on the march to find fodder existing only in their presumed destinations. Were there grasses along the path taken by horses to their final locations? Why did they not follow the path humans and marsupials took to Australia? Scientific creationists and diluviologists need to provide evidence in the form of survivors and fossils that such journeys had in fact taken place. Woodmorappe (1999: 11) ignores these issues and concludes his article by saying:

> The Creation model not only explains the distribution of living things on earth, but is also scientifically superior to the evolution model. This is because the creation model is more parsimonious. For example, it is much simpler to explain the similarities between the Australian and certain South American marsupials in terms of anthropogenic introductions after the Flood than it is to accept their evolution, over millions of years, while the continents drifted.

Another puzzle involving Australian marsupials deals with their variety. Variation itself need not challenge scientific creationists since they claim numerous types reflect the creator's wishes. The puzzle is that Australian marsupials resemble animals in other areas of the world in terms of the ecological niches they inhabit. There is a Tasmanian marsupial "wolf" that looked like a dog and was an aggressive predator. The bandicoot looks and acts like the European rabbit; there are also marsupial "mice" and "moles." The wombats are very much an equivalent to squirrels found elsewhere; the koala lives very much like the sloth (Colbert, 1985: 257). The issue is why these marsupials resemble animals found in other continents and why God did not use the same animals if their environments were the same. Evolutionists explain that marsupial mammals evolved to occupy these ecological niches because Australia was empty of placental mammals and the two types of mammals did not have to compete with one another.

The "anthropogenic introduction" of animals throughout the world is a common belief among Young-Earth scientific creationists. Ken Ham's children's book *Dinosaurs of Eden* (2001) shows a skin-clad man leading a stegoceras dinosaur carrying a pack (p. 43). In the same work, a drawing of the migration from the Tower of Babel shows a woman and child being carried by a gallimimus and a woman in a cart being drawn by a tsintaosaurus (p. 42). A similar book for children shows Adam and Eve with a dinosaur in the background (Morris and Ham, 1990: 16–17).

The migration patterns of birds offer little support for the dispersion theories of scientific creationists. Only one bird, the common crane of southern Russia, migrates from its Russian home to an area near Mount Ararat. Scientific creationists do not explain why no other birds migrate back to their former homes in Turkey. Robert A. Moore (1983: 17) asks whether God programmed birds to reach the ark before the flood at a specific time and then deprogrammed them so the surviving birds would not return to the ark after the flood. Perhaps God later reprogrammed birds to follow other migratory paths. The Rivoli's hummingbird winters in Mexico and the United States and summers in Nicaragua. Creationists need to explain why certain birds and fish follow their migration patterns and why they do not migrate to Mount Ararat or nearby areas.

There are other problems with the dispersals of animals from the ark. For example, many animals live in caves and cannot survive exposure to light and changes in environment. How did sightless cave-living species reach the ark? How did they find new caves after the deluvian cataclysms (Moore, 1983: 18)?

Noah and his relatives presumably carried various diseases existing only in humans, including five types of venereal diseases. Satan could have later created venereal diseases though that would give Satan creative powers. A creationist explanation is that venereal illnesses emerged because of the sins of post-flood people. If so, the process must have been similar to that of evolutionary processes or an act of creation that, according to creationist theology, was impossible after first six days of creation. Nor does the creationist model explain why some diseases are only found in limited geographic areas after evolutionary and adaptive processes are rejected.

Another set of unanswered questions deals with the survival of fish and other sea creatures. According to creationists, fish fossils were formed by drowning, similar to all other fossils. The turbulent oceans during the flood presumably contained silt and mud that clogged gills and suffocated fish. Many other sea creatures died as mountains rose and fell and continents shifted to their current positions. The salt content of the oceans must have changed. How did fresh water fish survive their new saltwater environment? By the same token, how did saltwater fish survive a change in salinity levels? Ken Ham (1999: 33) feels pre-flood fish contained genes enabling them to survive changes in salt levels. This genetic information, Ham guesses, has been lost in modern fish. This is another plausible argument that cannot be tested and must be accepted on faith.

In a related issue, the numerous volcanic eruptions taking place during the flood must have placed acids into the waters. These acids would have killed the fish that survived the changes in salt levels and the additional pollution of the waters due to silt, etc. Anti-creationists also ask how sea creatures could have survived the rise in water temperatures due to the volcanic eruptions forming the post-flood contours of the earth's landmasses.

Legends of the Ark

There exists a treasury of myths about observing the remains of the ark, and dedicated creationist arkeologists discuss the ark in one aspect or another. Finding the ark has been an industry almost as extensive as the search for the Loch Ness Monster in Scotland. Secondhand stories tell of a number of explorers who have seen, located, and entered the ark. Unfortunately, their film evidence is lost and their photographs too blurred for recognition. Legend has it that Czar Alexander sent an expedition to locate the ark after a Russian pilot had seen in 1916 what he described as a large wooden vessel on Mount Ararat (Chick, 1976: 24–5). The Czar sent an expedition of one hundred and fifty engineers and specialists and one hundred members of the expedition reached, photographed, and entered the ark (They found pens large enough to hold large dinosaurs (Chick, 1976: 25)). The Communists reportedly destroyed the documents after gaining power in Russia. The story of the Russian expedition was retracted later by a number of magazines that had published accounts of the expedition. The author of the original story admitted that it was mostly fiction (Moore, 1981: 8) though creationist Chick (1976) still reports it as evidence of the ark's existence.

There have been other alleged ark sightings though no physical evidence has been produced. American and Russian pilots claimed to have seen the ark in 1943. The American pilots reputedly took photographs, one of which was said to have been published in the Mediterranean edition of *Stars and Stripes* (Berlitz, 1987: 42). According to scientific creationists, the prints were lost though Charles Berlitz claims to have interviewed the deputy commander of the base from which the U.S. pilots flew. The former First Lieutenant states (Berlitz, 1987: 45):

> A Turkish pilot told us that the Ark was on the side of the mountain. It seemed logical to me. We took a bunch of flights around the area, looking at

castles and ruins, and then on Ararat we saw something different. It was about two-thirds of the way up the mountain, made of wood, and it looked like a boat or a wooden boat-shaped wall. I don't know who first said it was Noah's Ark. We all discussed it. Most of us felt it could be, since that's where it's supposed to be.

Mount Ararat guide Arslan is also quoted as stating (Berlitz, 1987: 69):

I believe enough people have seen it within the last fifty or sixty years to establish the truth of the [ark's] legend. It will probably be found right where it is supposed to be—between 14,000 and 15,000 feet up, following the right-hand side of Ahora Gorge right up to the front of the Parrot Glacier. There is a huge flat plateau there, as big as a football field, a hundred yards deep in ice. This is where, during melting periods, the Ark has been seen and pieces of it have been taken away, and this is where the remains of the Ark will be found.

There have been additional reports of finding rusty metal rivets on the slopes of Mount Ararat. This suggests to Kent E. Hovind and others that the ark was bolted together with metal parts to make it seaworthy (Hovind, n.d.). No one, however, has brought back any of these alleged metal parts for more intensive examinations.

Summary

The arguments put forth by scientific creationists to complete the limited description of the ark and a Noachian worldwide flood provided in the Bible illustrate the difficulty of forcing science and scripture together. It is impossible to patch together religious scripture and scientific evidence in any convincing and objective manner and attempts to do so violate the rules of evidence characterizing good science. When these implausible explanations fail to convince, scientific creationists call on divine intervention to explain discrepancies between scripture and evidence. Explaining the unexplainable in this way stifles the kind of careful inquiry that has helped us to better understand the world. Every public school curriculum trying to instill in students a correct view of science necessitates the rejection of scientific creationism as proper science.

The next chapter offers the latest attempts of scientific creationists to gain acceptance into orthodox scientific circles. For the last decade, a new type of scientific creationist, called intelligent designers, has focused on the assumption that life is too complicated to have emerged through evolutionary processes and therefore the existence of life demands recognition of a creator. Proponents of intelligent design have abandoned the attempts to reconcile scripture and science and focus on the inadequacies of science itself to provide a complete understanding of the emergence and development of life.

Intelligent Design

There is no more reason to believe that man descended from some inferior animal than there is to believe that a stately mansion had descended from a small cottage.

—*William Jennings Bryan*

What is Intelligent Design?

The argument from design has been a core argument for the existence of a creator from the early Christian era to the present. The modern version of the intelligent design (ID) position continues the belief in the existence of a deity perceived through observation of the natural world. Although ID proponents are vague as to what this intelligence could be and they claim their position is not theistic, the scope and complexity of nature's designs suggest an unspecified creator.

Intelligent design has two major related characteristics. First, IDers claim that organisms are too complex to have evolved according to evolutionary principles. The presence of such complexity can be fully explained only by acknowledging a supernatural agent must have created life. Second, IDers attack orthodox science as limited to naturalistic phenomena. They claim, as do philosophers in general, that orthodox science (called methodological naturalism) eliminates the inclusion of the supernatural. According to intelligent design theorists, orthodox scientists wrongly limit their studies to natural phenomena without considering any other alternatives such as the supernatural. Intelligent design proponents argue it is wrong to eliminate the possibility of a creator and that the addition of design in scientific analyses offers answers naturalistic scientists mistakenly reject.

The complexity of life suggests to IDers that a creator is necessary in any attempt to understand the origin and diversity of life. Any naturalistic model of life, such as evolution, is *de facto* incomplete and inadequate unless it includes a supernatural element. Scientific creationists John Ankerberg and John Weldon

(1998: 226) succinctly challenge the evolutionary model when they state "...if evolution is to be considered a true scientific fact, it must be able to explain the origin of developed life forms by recourse to proven methods of evolutionary change." They, of course, ignore or reject the evidence that meets this challenge.

The main thrust of intelligent design theorists, however, is to attack evolutionary theories by saying organisms are too complex to have evolved in a natural fashion. If so, then an alternative explanation for the variety of life is the existence of a supernatural creator. This sets the stage for a plea that scientific creationism should be presented to students as a better alternative to the evolutionary model.

Acceptance of design, however, logically leads to the implicit acceptance that design can only originate from a supernatural entity. Intelligent designers argue they can prove nature is too complex to exist without a creator and that evolutionary forces could never develop living organisms through a random process. How one defines this supernatural creator/designer is irrelevant to the central intelligent design tenet that nature is too complex to involve evolutionary processes.

The reluctance of specifying what IDers mean by a supernatural designer is a retreat from the Biblical literalism of scientific creationists. For this reason, though intelligent design emerged from scientific creationism, the former forms a distinct category of creationism. ID proponents ignore Biblical literalism and the Bible itself because of the failures to use science to buttress religious beliefs. In addition, Young-Earth creationism contains too many beliefs obviously contradicting established scientific findings, observations, and common sense. As a result, the contemporary intelligent design school is a rejection of traditional forms of creationism (Kitcher, 2001: 258). A person can accept the intelligent design arguments without accepting the non-empirical baggage scientific creationists carry. While scientific creationists constantly use the design argument, intelligent design creationists avoid discussing any other theological material except design itself. The design argument as intelligent designers present it suggests scientific creationism is no longer an attractive argument to many creationists (Van Till, 2001: 489).

The intelligent design argument is gaining support among a wide range of scientific creationists although Dr. Leonard Krishtalka, director of the University of the Kansas Natural History Museum and Biodiversity Research Center describes intelligent design as "nothing more than creationism dressed in a cheap tuxedo (Glanz, 2001). This stance ignores the attraction of the intelligent design argument. Intelligent design is now in the forefront among critics of the evolutionary model.

Intelligent design supporters insist they observe nature in an impartial manner and their religious views are irrelevant. Michael J. Behe challenges orthodox scientists to understand life in a similar impartial manner (Behe, 2000: 127):

> I have written that if you look at molecular machines, such as the cilium, the flagellum, and others, they look like they were designed—purposely designed by an intelligent agent...I think the conclusion of intelligent design in these cases is completely empirical. That is, it is based entirely on the physical evidence, along with an understanding of how we come to conclude that an object was designed.

It is important to note any consideration of design in nature implies both a designer and a plan/purpose. These central characteristics imply a theistic orientation. A case in point is Dean L. Overman's argument for design (1997). Overman's orientation is philosophical and he demonstrates it is impossible for life and the universe to have begun through random processes. He states self-organization (the beginning of life) has too great a "mathematical impossibility" to be believable; that "an objective, reasonable person who follows mathematical and other logical thought processes and the principles of the scientific method will not favor a proposition which has a very low probability...;" the Miller and Urey experiments are falsely interpreted; plus additional arguments. However, in spite of Overman's arguments, he concludes his book with a theistic evolutionary position (Overman, 1997: 197):

> Life cannot be explained by an appeal to accident; and if life transcends the laws of physics and chemistry, then the origin of life will never be demonstrated by an adequate self-organization scenario...If life transcends the laws of physics and chemistry, then a rational conclusion is that a Person, not chance and the laws of physics and chemistry, caused and is causing life.

Overman is open about adding to his logical analyses that a supernatural entity (an unspecified Person) created and continues to create life, though he does not support this claim. Not all intelligent designers are so honest, but their analyses necessarily point to a deity of some, usually unspecified, type (see also Dembski, 2002: 351).

A number of physicists and chemists disagree with the above statements. Nobel Laureate Christian de Duve (1995) finds that life at all levels emerged and developed because chemical and physical laws create order and increasing complexity, as found naturally among crystals. In the same manner, Cairns-Smith

(1985) hypothesizes certain clays could have provided the first structures allowing the start of life. Cairns-Smith (see also Strahler, 1999: 515–24) notes certain clays, such as kaolin, are chemically active because they carry a negative electrical charge to attract macronutrients. Such clays are found in mud and dark soils, and can hold water as well as attract iron, calcium, and other minerals in ion form to develop early forms of life.

Two Early Intelligent Design Theorists

Mary Roberts (1788–1865) and William Paley (1743–1805) are two early modern examples of intelligent designers. While their design arguments differ in major details, both described how nature proved the existence of a divine creator.

Mary Roberts published a large number of biographies and books on natural history (Gould, 1995: 193). She was a conventional naturalist for her era but was very eloquent in her description of a divine creator whose work culminated in human beings (Gould, 1995: 193):

> All the various parts of nature are beautifully designed to act in concert. We see the hand of God employed in forming the lowest, and frequently, in our opinion, the most despicable creatures; assigning to each its station and so admirably adjusting the mighty whole, that every particle of matter, and every living thing that creeps, or moves, upon the surface of the earth, is formed in subserviency to the general good.

Roberts's writings reflect the comforting Victorian view nature is ordered and its social hierarchies pre-ordained. The apex and purpose of this order of course is humanity, at least its more advanced representatives, meaning the British upper and middle classes. The universe, Roberts continues, was a moral one that also established a hierarchy of social classes and relations. One fear of anti-Darwinists during the 1800s was that Darwinism suggested persons were equal to one another. Darwinism challenged the comforting view of universal purpose and goodness by stressing a universal struggle for survival during which species come into existence without external purpose or direction. They then become extinct through no fault of their own except inadequate adaptation to changing environmental conditions. Roberts' view of life was essentially a conservative one in which the social hierarchy was divinely ordained. Any change in the natural order (including democracy, social equality, and revolution) violated the creator's intent and purpose. The Darwinian model of impersonal change due to adaptation or lack of it disturbed many persons then and still does today. A major criticism of evolutionary models by contemporary scientific creationists is that Darwinism in all of its forms rejects the existence of a moral universe containing absolute standards.

The most influential proponent of the intelligent design (ID) argument during the nineteenth century was William Paley. His *Natural Theology, or Evidences of the Existence and Attributes of the Deity Collected from the Appearance of Nature*, first published in 1802, offers a traditional "argument from design" that the complexity and interdependence of living organisms "proves" the existence of a creator/designer which must be the Biblical God. Paley's arguments remain forceful defenses of creationism among contemporary creationists and Paley can be considered as a scientific creationist in his analysis and extensive observation of nature (Thompson, 2003: 12). Paley's *Natural Theology* had a great impact during the first part of the nineteenth century. Charles Darwin read Paley's work as an undergraduate and was impressed by Paley's theistic argument from design. Paley was not especially original, but his style of presentation and the many examples of what he understood as proof of intelligent design proved successful. This book was so convincing that it allowed the young Darwin to decide he could honestly profess a belief in a Christian God should he decide to take religious orders.

Paley enjoyed the respect of students, clergy, and intellectuals alike until various forms of evolution became accepted, although Paley's argument retains a central importance in scientific creationists' arguments against evolution. Paley argued life is functional—there is a purpose to all living parts: eyes exist to provide vision, etc. Paley also argued that organisms, which are composed of many complex parts such as eyes, are further proof of an intelligent designer at work. Using a methodology similar to the one used by Darwin in *The Origin of Species* and later works, Paley collected an overwhelming number of cases to prove his point a creator assembled the universe and the complex bodies of organisms. His major work, *Natural Theology*, contains the most powerful analogy in the scientific creationist argument for intelligent design. Paley begins his book with this impressive passage (Paley, 1900 [1802]):

> In crossing a heath, suppose I pitched my foot against a *stone*, and were asked how the stone came to be there, I might possibly answer, that for any thing I knew to the contrary it had lain there for ever, nor would it, perhaps, be very easy to show the absurdity of this answer. But suppose I had found a *watch* upon the ground, and it should be inquired how the watch happened to be in that place, I should hardly think of the answer which I had before given, that for any thing I know the watch might have always been there. Yet why should

not this answer serve for the watch as well as for the stone; why is it not as admissible in the second case as in the first? For this reason, and for no other, namely, that when we come to inspect the watch, we perceive—what we could not discover in the stone—that its several parts are framed and put together for a purpose...that if the different parts had been differently shaped from what they are, or placed after any other manner or in any other order than that in which they are placed, either no motion at all would have been carried on in the machine, or none which would have answered the use that is now served by it.

Roman author and philosopher Cicero earlier used Paley's example of a watch as proof of design in 45 B.C. In his work *The Nature of the Gods*, Cicero asks, "When we see a mechanism such as a planetary model or a clock, do we doubt that it is the work of a conscious intelligence? So how can we doubt that the world is the work of the divine intelligence?" (quote in Case-Winter, 2000: 70) Design as proof of a creator was also a central concept of Thomas Aquinas (1225–1274), in large part because only God could be the prime (first) mover. Contemporary creationists in general use the design argument in one form or another.

According to Leonard Brand (1997), the notion of design through supernatural means need not be anti-scientific and he suggests intelligent designers first treat phenomena in an objective manner. However, Brand continues, proponents of intelligent design could then hypothesize God has intervened in natural processes and then prove their case (Brand, 1997: 66–7). Brand begins with the assumption that the Bible is a valid source of naturalistic knowledge (1997: 68):

> ...the Designer communicated to us and evidence indicates the communication is reliable in describing the actual history of life. The communication is brief; it leaves many unanswered questions. But if it is a reliable account, the most productive approach will be to take it seriously and see what insights its concepts can give us in our research. Statements from the book cannot be used as evidence in science; but if those statements are true, we should be able to use some of them as a basis for defining hypotheses that lead to productive research.

To date, there has been no "productive research" based on information from the Bible or on the assumption that a creator/designer exists. In spite of the claims of intelligent design supporters such as Brand, ID cannot be a source of research if the answer to a specific question or hypothesis is always "God did it." Such a research agenda was first proposed by George McCready during the 1930s (see chapter four), but has not yet presented any convincing and original finding. Intelligent design theorists also propose a "God of the gaps" answer to all complexities not understood by evolutionists: God—or a vaguely defined supernatural intelligence—is used as an explanation for phenomena not explained by orthodox science. ID supporters accuse evolutionists of also accepting gaps in evolutionary knowledge and that in consequence use a form of secular faith to support their beliefs in evolution. Theistic scientists do the same when they include a supernatural agency in their theoretical frameworks (Moreland, 1994).

Criticisms of Intelligent Design

Philip Frymire is a careful critic of scientific creationism as presented in the works of scientific creationist Phillip E. Johnson. Frymire (2000) criticizes the intelligent design group by asking what proof there is in design in nature. Design implies a purpose although intelligent designers do not suggest what that purpose is or how independent investigators could discover this purpose. More traditional scientific creationists are willing to state what the purpose of nature is and what the origin of this purpose can be. An example of the scientific creationists' use of purpose is the question why stars exist (Batten, 2000: 143–44):

> The reason stars were made are given to us in several places in the Bible...God made the stars for mankind on earth, not for another alien race "out there." Add to this the sequence of creation...and it is easy to see the thrusts of the Biblical testimony, that the purpose of creation is uniquely centered on this earth.

There is no possibility the purpose(s) of design would be interpreted other than that the universe having been created for mankind on the part of ID proponents. Nevertheless, scientific creationists believe that intelligent design is a scientific alternative to evolutionary theory and should be taught as a valid part of scientific curricula (Davis and Kenyon, 1993). Gilchrist (1997), however, has shown that intelligent design researchers have totally ignored intelligent design as a guide to their own research. This suggests ID cannot aid in developing new knowledge.

The hidden goal of intelligent design theorists is to provide a "wedge" to include a discussion of the supernatural in science curricula. Doing so, they hope, would cause students to reject the naturalistic evolutionary model taught in science courses and replace it with the scientific creationist model. William Dembski, a leading intelligent design theorist, is clear on the goal of intelligent designers (quoted in Forrest, 2001: 30):

> Intelligent Design opens the whole possibility of us being created in the image of a benevolent God...The job of apologetics is to clear the ground, to clear obstacles that prevent people from coming to the knowledge of Christ...And if there's anything that I think has blocked the growth of Christ as the free reign of the Spirit and people accepting the Scripture and Jesus Christ, it is the Darwinian naturalistic view...It's important that we understand the world. God has created it; Jesus is incarnate in the world.

Niles Eldredge (2000: 141) and Richard Dawkins (1996: 141) correctly point out the argument from design proves very little by itself since the assertion that some processes in nature are too complex to be natural is theological rather than logical. This leads to the assumption a supernatural entity or entities must exist to accomplish what nature could not while also implying limits to both natural processes and scientific investigations. In other words, nature contains mysteries beyond the minds of researchers to understand.

Intelligent design advocates present another argument in addition to the assertion that complexity demands a designer. Darwinians state that evolution proceeds slowly and randomly. Evolutionary processes operate on a random basis although each new step builds on past developments. Intelligent design proponents create a straw man in their assertion that physical complexities cannot emerge randomly. Precipitating events may be random, but structural change accumulates step-by-step. Intelligent designers reject the notion that physical complexities can emerge in a random fashion, a view best offered by James Perloff (1999: 70):

> We can drop sugar, flour, baking powder, and an egg on the floor—but they won't turn into a cake by themselves. We have to mix and bake them according to a recipe. Throwing steel, rubber, glass and plastic together doesn't make a car. It takes skillful engineering. How much more, then, would intelligence be needed to design life?

The intelligent design approach is undergoing much criticism as research continually explains the development of increasingly complex organs and biochemical processes. An example of such discoveries is a study of how the heart developed. In 1993, Ralf Bodmer discovered the *tinman* gene determining the development of the heart of the fruit fly (Zimmer, 2000: 58). *Tinman* and another gene, *Nkx*, are similar to a third gene found in nematode worms that have throat muscles. The hypothesis is that a gene controlling the development of throat muscles was duplicated in a different part of a worm's body and began to pump blood rather than food. Gradually, other new genes emerged later to control the development of more complex multi-chambered hearts (Zimmer, 2000: 59).

It has been hypothesized that multi-chambered hearts developed from genes controlling other but similar functions. The point is that nature did not have to develop multi-chambered hearts from scratch in a bit-by-bit process. Instead, complex hearts developed quickly from the building blocks of master genes controlling the development of other body parts. In a similar fashion, Mark Fishman discovered roughly a dozen heart-module genes, each of which controls one aspect or another of a zebrafish's heart (Zimmer, 2000). Some could be used to control growth in other areas. These "additions" indicate that evolution is not random but builds on existing structures.

The Issue of Eyes and Other Complex Organs

Similar to intelligent design supporters today, both Paley and Darwin used eyes as examples of complexity. Darwin (1979), in the sixth chapter of *The Origin of Species*, graded vision organs from simple to complex in structure and function. Paley on his part claimed the eye is "too subtle for our discernment or something else besides the known laws of mechanism taking place...(Paley, 1900: 21–2)." In the quote above, Paley claims no one can completely discover how the eye sees; he is willing to admit to both a supernatural intervention, i.e. a creator, as the originator of the eye and to a limitation to scientific investigation.

Contemporary scientific creationists continue to state the probability complex structures such as an eye can develop into useful organs is too low to be believable (Dembski, 1999). It is as believable (and as impossibly likely) that a "tornado in a junkyard," to quote the title of book by scientific creationist James Perloff (1999), could produce a working jumbo airliner. Perloff also notes airliners are made up of parts that cannot fly until assembled. They all have to be present in a specific combination to make flight possible; an evolutionary process adding one new feature at a time would not result in a viable organism (see also Hamilton, 1991) since the additions would not be useful until all were present.

Evolutionists admit they do not know yet how complex biological structures evolved, though recent research points to a number of promising directions. They nevertheless reject the intelligent designers' conclusions. Evolutionists such as Chris McGowan (1984: 45) agree with scientific creationists that complicated structures cannot evolve spontaneously. No evolutionist accepts the notion that, for example, a 400-animo acid protein molecule emerged whole in an instant purely by chance. However, it is logically acceptable to hypothesize that a simple molecule gradually became more and more complex or joined with others to perform new functions. McGowan continues his argument that biological processes contain structure and new combinations and additions can only occur in limited pathways. There are, McGowan states, laws of physics and biochemistry limiting developmental and evolutionary processes (see Dawkins, 1996: 11 and 171). These limited pathways increase the probabilities IDers assume are too low to consider possible.

Intelligent designers present another argument forcefully presented by Michael J. Behe (1996). Behe, a molecular biologist, notes that many biological processes are closed systems in which all parts depend on one another to exist and function. For example, cell membranes require proteins in order to develop and function. At the same time, proteins need cell membranes to function. One part of the cell cannot function without the others, and one could not "evolve" before the others. On the other hand, the probability proteins, cell membranes, and genes carrying the information for their development evolved at the same time is difficult to accept by both creationists and evolutionists (Perloff, 1999: 72). On this point the two intellectual divisions agree with one another.

Intelligent design advocates cannot explain many aspects of the natural world. For example, they have not yet explained nature's cruelty. Evolutionists explain pain, suffering, and violent death in nature as the result of competition for survival. There is an "arms race" between prey and victim as to who will survive longer. This "problem of evil" among presumably sinless organisms has been a concern among philosophers and natural theologians. Intelligent design defenders must face the question why the designer exhibits such a cruel nature.

The ichneumon fly's (actually a wasp) procreative strategies have been used both as an illustration of nature's harshness and as a rejection of the view nature has a moral element reflecting a concerned creator. The logic of intelligent design forces adherents to accept the working hypothesis that ichneumon's behavior is a miracle designed by a creator. A possible creationist explanation for the ichneumon behavior is that the fly selects hosts that harm crops useful to humans and therefore the victim's fate indicates a benevolent and caring attitude toward humans. Charles Lyell (1797–1875) presented this defense though his theories in geology provided Darwin with the idea of slow organic changes during geological eons. An alternative explanation is that Satan or evil forces created the ichneumoniodea and similar species as a result of Adam and Eve's fall from grace, though this explanation gives more power to the forces of evil than many creationists are willing to accept.

Ichneumon larvae feed on hosts until they become mobile and able to survive as independent organisms (Gould, 1983: 32–34). There are a number of ways to ensure the survival of the ichneumon eggs. Some species pierce their victims' bodies and deposit eggs inside the bodies. The larvae hatch inside the host's body and gradually eat the soft interior. Other ichneumon species lay eggs on the outside of a host and at the same time inject a paralyzing toxin. The victim, usually a caterpillar, remains alive and immobile and cannot dislodge or harm the eggs. The larvae eat the digestive organs first, thereby leaving the heart and central nervous system to maintain the life of the body. It would otherwise decay and become useless to the larvae developing inside if the body died (Gould, 1983: 35).

Charles Darwin (1958 [1892]) used the example of the ichneumon as an example of the fallacy of seeing nature's complexity as the work of a creator/designer. In a letter to Asa Grey written in 1860, Darwin responded to an attack on evolution by a minister. Darwin says (1958: 249):

> But I own that I cannot see as plainly as others do, and as I should wish to do, evidence of design and beneficence on all sides of us. There seems to me too much misery in the world. I cannot persuade myself that a beneficent and omnipotent God would have designedly created the Ichneumonidae with the express intention of their feeding within the living bodies of caterpillars, or that a cat should play with mice. Not believing this, I see no necessity in the belief that the eye was expressly designed.

The creation of the cuckoo can be just as easily questioned. Cuckoos lay eggs in other birds' nests and the cuckoo hatchling is always larger than its foster siblings. It can either push the smaller birds out of the nest, receive more food, or both. Defenders of intelligent design approach have yet to explain nature's propensity of tooth and claw. Evolutionists such as Stephen Jay Gould take the position there is no evidence of morality or ultimate meaning in nature. If nature were designed with a purpose as they claim, ID theorists have the responsibility to explain the purpose of tapeworms, malaria, and a host of other organisms painful to humans and other living organisms.

Other creationists, some of whom are theistic evolutionists, have proposed that God allows independence in his creations. Evil (i.e. suffering) is the result of the behavior of organisms rather than part of a pre-determined design. Process theologians such as Alfred North Whitehead (1861–1947) and his followers accept the proposition God has a purpose for his creations to which he allows freedom of action. Scientific creationists respond that while there is a purpose to God's creations, suffering is the result of sin. Other creationists suggest suffering is caused in part by active satanic forces.

Human Backbones, Eyes, and Other Issues

The human backbone and eye are topics commonly argued by evolutionary and intelligent design supporters. Evolutionists claim that spines and eyes are badly designed because they are the result of processes formed through minute steps. Proponents of intelligent design reject the possibilities of both less-than-ideal design and step-by-step development. Human spines evolved from those of fish, to amphibians, to mammals, to primates, and finally to humans, yet the major evolutionary structural change in terms of the spine took place when proto-humans developed the ability to walk upright. Spines originally developed for four-legged locomotion demanded structural compromises before walking on two legs became possible.

The backbone went from a single-curve arch into an S-curve (Krogman, 1951). The lower section became weaker and thinner and the pelvis became thicker to bear heavier loads. These changes created increased pressure on the spine, resulting in higher likelihood of low and high back pains, hernias, and slipped disks.

The added height when standing resulted in more work for the heart to pump blood from feet to head and also resulted in a greater likelihood of varicose veins. Other parts of the body also became casualties to make it possible to stand upright (Krogman, 1951). Back problems, fallen-arches, bunions, calluses, and other foot miseries hark back to the fact that our spines and feet have not yet (if ever) developed through evolutionary selection into really efficient units.

Olshanksy and colleagues (2001) suggested a number of physical changes that would be useful for humans reaching old age. An increased number of ribs would decrease the likelihood of organ damage and would also decrease the likelihood of hernias. Shorter stature and more valves in leg veins would reduce the development of varicose veins and blood pooling. The male prostate gland and the female bladder could also be redesigned to prevent obstruction of the flow of urine and incontinence, respectively. Other improvements can easily be imagined. However, evolutionary processes made our bodies imperfect rather than the result of sin as scientific creationists argue.

Intelligent design theorists ignore human frailty and focus on the positive side of creation. Arthur Custance presents an effective example of the marvel of design (1972: 261):

> The whole body of man has, therefore, clearly been designed to support and enhance the uniqueness of his mind. Mind, tongue, and hand have somehow been structured in a very remarkable way to give coordinated expression to the sum total of human potential: to the power of reflection, of communication, and of creation; in fact, at one and the same time, of having dominion over the rest of God's creation and yet of worshiping the Creator.

Custance's phrase "having dominion" is similar to the highest place in nature's hierarchy given humans by earlier creationists such as Mary Roberts. There is little in scientific creationism or in intelligent design that is new.

IDers reject the notion of vestigial organs that often cause problems to their wearers. IDers argue an object does not have to be perfect to be recognized as having a design (Geilser and Anderson, 1987: 160). IDers do not, however, continue the logic of their argument to discuss the nature of a god that creates imperfect organisms and seemingly useless and badly formed parts.

Nevertheless, intelligent designers feel that life and the structure of organisms are too well organized to have developed bit by bit without design. Geisler and Anderson (1987: 163) use the analogy of a play by Shakespeare. All of the words in the play can be found in the dictionary, but it takes an intelligence to place the words together to create a meaningful play. Evolutionists answer that evolution is not random because evolution proceeds from one small step to another to slowly develop more complicated organisms. Intelligent designers respond the probability that life could emerge from simple materials and continuously develop demands too large probabilities. Geisler and Anderson ask how randomness could turn the simple phrase "Mary had a little lamb" into the more complex epic *Paradise Lost.*

Dembski (1999: 143) proposes the objective definition of design as a very small probability of occurrence. In essence, he wishes to determine which parts of nature are miraculous using a probability model. By contrast, evolutionists claim all complex biological phenomena developed in "gradual evolution stages by natural selection (Dawkins, 1996: 37)." Dembski and other intelligent designers mistakenly assume whatever is currently unexplained is by fiat unexplainable, and therefore proof of design (Scott, 2001: 2258). However, the history of science offers numerous examples of advances in knowledge and no one should assume what is presently unexplained should be explained by a supernatural agency. In addition, evolutionists are aware their knowledge is incomplete; lack of knowledge does not demand non-physical explanations. Instead, ignorance is a spur for further research and indicates a theory is incomplete rather than false.

Michael Behe (1996: 31–6) and other ID advocates present the example of the bombardier beetle as proof of design in organisms. This beetle sprays a toxic substance at scalding temperatures when threatened by predators. It produces and stores hydrogen peroxide and hydroquinone in separate compartments. The chemicals are sent to a third compartment from which is secreted enzyme catalysts. The hydrogen peroxide breaks down into water and oxygen. The water reacts with the hydroquinone to produce heat and a toxic chemical called quinone. The resulting steam creates pressure and the mixture is propelled through a sphincter onto whatever threatens the beetle. The potential predator is sprayed with a toxic, smelly liquid that is also scalding. Behe argues each sequential part is useless without the others because they all must be present before they can be used as a defense.

Behe asks how evolution could have possibly developed the defense mechanism of the beetle in a step-by-step fashion. Duane T. Gish (1978: 512) similarly asks how intermediate bombardier beetles could have evolved partial defenses useless until all parts of the defense system were present. All parts of its defense need to be present or they are either useless or dangerous to the beetle. Scientific creationist Robert E. Kofahl (1981: 14) asks why such a complex system is needed at all since numerous beetles use glands to secrete bad tasting or toxic chemical mixtures:

> Of course, until controlled explosions became possible to the beetle, there would be no need for the amiable orifices or guns that are now attached to the vestibules of the beetle. So we might speculate that the earlier forms of beetles of the genus *Brachinus* used shotguns which were not very efficient. Greater efficiency was gained by evolving the shotgun barrels into rifle barrels. Then the beetle could shoot his enemies by aiming his rear end at them and pulling a trigger mechanism which he had just happened to evolve in the nick of time...It does seem to me that to believe such a scenario is credible requires strong faith in the capabilities of atoms and science, but those who believe in evolution have such a faith. Those who believe in creation likewise have strong faith. The difference is that they place their faith in a Being of infinite intelligence and power whose intelligent, purposeful designs are evident everywhere in nature.

The argument above includes most of the themes used by ID advocates: the argument from complexity, the accusation that evolution is a matter of faith, and that complexity cannot be understood without a creator. Christopher Gregory Weber (1981) answers Kofahl's criticisms. He notes other beetles use the same chemicals for defense as do the Bombardier Beetle and the addition of a spraying mechanism would not be impossible under the evolutionary framework though he admits he has not proven his explanations. Weber concludes that his scenario of the beetle's development makes no sense under the rubric of creationism and that his hypothesis is the start of the analysis of how the defense mechanism evolved. By contrast, acceptance of the creationist approach ends all further speculation and study since the acceptance of a designed miracle explains everything. Weber did not directly answer Kofahl's criticisms except to say the occurrence of evolution is well established while the mechanisms of evolution are not yet understood.

Michael Behe convincingly presents the example of a mousetrap to explain the concept of complexity as the result of design. Though a simple mechanism, a mousetrap cannot become effective (functional) until all parts are present. Thus, a simple mousetrap is irreducibly complex and must be designed *in toto* by a designer with a final purpose in mind, in this case to catch mice. Behe feels this concept *irreducible complexity* is a revolutionary idea thoroughly discrediting evolutionary theory and proves the purposeful design in biological structures. Behe proudly states (Behe, 1996: 232–3) in probably one of the most arrogant statements made recently by a scientist that:

> The result of these cumulative efforts to investigate the cell—to investigate life at the molecular level—is a loud, clear, piercing cry of "*design!*" The result is so unambiguous and so significant that it must be ranked as one of the greatest achievements in the history of science. The discovery rivals those of Newton and Einstein, Lavoisier and Schrödenger, Pasteur and Darwin. The observation of the intelligent design of life is as momentous as the observation that the earth goes around the sun or that disease is caused by bacteria or that radiation is emitted in quanta.

Behe notes after the quote above that scientists have ignored this "significant" finding. He seems surprised few have taken the concept of irreducible complexity seriously. Behe and other scientific creationists offer no proof of the validity that biological complexity demands a creator/designer. Yet the argument of irreducible complexity is a powerful and attractive strategy that adds to the theistic argument from design.

Although the ID arguments are emotionally attractive, they ignore several elements of nature apart from nature's cruelty and the presence of imperfect and useless structures. Intelligent design does not explain, except by appealing to God's whim, why there are so many variations of basic designs that make no sense except within the evolutionary framework. Darwin's first understanding of evolutionary principles occurred in the Galápagos Islands. He discovered (after his return) he had collected fourteen different species of finches from nearby islands. The species were differentiated primarily by the shape and size of their beaks. One finch species had strong, thick beaks allowing members to crack open larger seeds plentiful on an island. Another species, located where insects were easily caught, had thin, sharp beaks allowing birds to pick insects out of the dirt. Members of a third species had beaks capable of holding small sticks in order to dig grubs from holes in trees (Sonder, 1999: 10–11).

Darwin hypothesized the Galápagos finches had common ancestors that originally had migrated from South America. These descendants adapted to their new island conditions by taking advantages of new sources of food and new ways of collecting food. Essentially, those finches able to take advantage of new sources of food were more likely to survive, have more progeny, and pass their genetic advantages to future generations. This reasoning became known as natural selection. One hundred years later, naturalists Peter and Rosemary Grant observed the same process among finches in the Galápagos Islands (Weiner, 1995). Defenders of the intelligent design argument offer little explanation for nature's variety except a supernatural cause.

Although Behe and other ID advocates are correct when they state structures of organisms are complex, there are questions to how "irreducibly complex" parts of organisms can be. Critics of intelligent design point out that many seemingly complex systems can be broken down into simpler sub-systems.

An aspect of evolution ignored by intelligent design advocates is the fact that genes undergo frequent duplications. The significance of gene duplication is that a duplicated gene can undergo mutation and develop new traits without endangering the original gene and its functions. That is, duplicated genes add to an organism's ability to change (Pennisi, 2000) without losing functions without which the organism dies. These duplicated genes can also form the basis of speciation by traveling to another chromosome or to another area of the genome. Such changes would allow for extensive physical changes, including forming new species (Lynch and Conery, 2000: 1151). While most gene duplications disappear, it appears some become permanent and have served as agents of evolution (Lynch and Conery, 2000: 1154).

Biologist Scott Person at *The Institute for Genomic Research* investigated the smallest number of genes necessary for life (Kintisch, 2001). The *Mycoplasma genetalium* is found in the human urogenital tract and evolved by discarding unneeded genes (and body parts) until it now has roughly a very small 470 genes because parasites lose the functions their hosts provide. As a comparison, another bacteria, the *Haemophilus influenzae*, has at least 1,700 genes. Peterson is manipulating the *Mycoplasma's* genes to discover the minimum number of genes necessary for its survival. The *mycoplasma* needs at least 200 genes to survive and Peterson is studying another 100 of its genes to see whether or not they are crucial for survival. Some of these "extra" genes could be used in evolutionary processes. Such work offers insights how evolution proceeds.

Summary

Intelligent design as a scientific strategy is an intellectual dead end in large part because the view of nature offered by intelligent designers is too simplistic. For example, intelligent designers claim feathers and eyes could not have developed because a partial eye or feather would not offer any survival advantages. ID proponents wrongly insist that new features must appear in their complete, final forms or not all. The implicit suggestion is that any complex feature such as a heart, eye, feather, limb, or blood clotting mechanism could only appear through a creative act. However, complex biological phenomena such as feathers or eyes can be useful to their organisms as simpler forms. If so, then simpler examples of complex parts of organisms could develop in a step-by-step process through natural selection while these intermediate stages remain evolutionary effective. An eye mechanism offering a ten percent improvement in light sensitivity—such as a light-sensitive skin patch—offers a better chance of survival than no patch at all.

The human eye, in addition, is useful and complex but it is not perfect and not all humans have optimum vision. This suggests the eye developed through evolutionary trial and error rather than through the creation of a supernatural designer. Journalist Carol Kaesuk Yoon (Wade, 1998: 174) notes that "Evolution produces the striking new by tinkering with the old." Evolution uses what is available and does not start fresh as scientific creationists and intelligent designers insist.

When their arguments fail to convince, IDers rely on the design-by-declaration rhetorical strategy by merely stating that intelligent design is correct, as the following assertion declares (Sarfati, 2003: 45):

At the time of writing, debate rages in Ohio, USA, abut whether there is 'design' in nature, or if the teaching of intelligent design is even 'science'. However, as shown, the best robotics engineers have yet to design a navigation program as good as a bee's and run it on a chip with the energy efficiency of a bee's brain. So it's reasonable to believe that the bee was designed by a Master Programmer whose intelligence is beyond our own.

In the end, intelligent design proponents rely on the argument that design in nature is "reasonable" and therefore evolutionary theory is incorrect.

On-going computer-based research shows that simple self-directing programs can develop complex structures and characteristics (Wolfram, 2002). Such work suggests simple structures can develop complex behaviors, contrary to the claims of ID proponents. In addition, experiments based on chaos theory indicate chaotic systems develop organization and structure. In this case, IDers are ignoring roughly thirty years of research offering another rejection for arguments supporting intelligent design.

The Future of Creationism

○ ○

The decree of evolution: what works survives; what does not work becomes extinct.

—Anon.

Current Strategies of Scientific Creationism in the Courtroom and Classroom

In 1987, the U. S. Supreme Court rejected a Louisiana Legislative Act requiring teachers to teach creationism if they taught evolution. To scientific creationists, fair play and logic demand scientific creationism be given equal treatment with the theory of evolution to create a "balance" by allowing each side of the controversy to present its case. Justice William Brennan rejected this argument and wrote the majority opinion that scientific creationism was an attempt "to achieve a religious purpose" by including scientific creationism in their curricula.

Scientific creationists are now searching for the right strategy to allow the teaching of creationism in public schools. One recently developed argument is that teachers should be given the independence of teaching "alternatives" to evolution (Boxer, 1987) if, under the provision of freedom of religion, their conscience demanded that they teach creationism. The Creation Science Legal Defense Fund was organized to protect the right of teachers to teach creationism if they wished.

Another current strategy of creationists is the "bottom-up" strategy involving attacks on the teaching of evolution through the support of creationist members of school boards and the harassment of teachers by students. Scientific creationists now also offer kits and pamphlets to students wishing to avoid exposure to class lectures with evolutionary contents. Following advice from one of these kits, a student rose from his seat, went to the back of the classroom, faced the wall, put fingers in his ears, and hummed when the teacher began to lecture on evolution!

There are church-sponsored seminars teaching students how to debate evolution-supporting statements made by their teachers. Ken Ham's *Answers in Genesis* organization offers lecture materials that criticize evolution and present the creationist position. There is even a PowerPoint presentation kit with almost four hundred slides for those wishing to lecture on creationist topics. The organization's twelve video series (available in DVD format) also contains very persuasive lectures by Ham.

Jack L. Chick recommends that students challenge their high school teachers as to the validity of evolutionary theories. In his anti-evolution tracts and comic books Chick offers specific guidelines, rhetorical advice, and topics with which to challenge evolutionary materials. Students should remain polite and respectful while they present anti-evolution arguments. In Chick's tract *Big Daddy?*, a student politely offers such overwhelming "proofs" evolution is an intellectual sham that the professor decides never to teach evolution again (Alston, 2002). In a similar strategy, Kent E. Hovind (n.d.) suggests in his video series that "It wouldn't hurt to be well dressed and groomed" before openly challenging a teacher's pro-evolutionary statements. Hovind, founder of *Creation Science Evangelism*, makes available a well-produced video *Creation Seminar Series* for church groups and other anti-evolution organizations to prepare students to resist evolutionary statements made in their schools.

The "bottom-up" classroom strategy of scientific creationists enabling students to challenge their teachers will increase in intensity since a growing number of churches include scientific creationism teaching modules in their youth programs. Their graduates will increasingly be vocal in their rejection of evolution in their high schools and universities.

The Need to Expose Teachers to Better Evolutionary Material

Scientific creationists are neither ignorant nor out of touch with the modern world and contemporary science as they were pictured seventy-five years ago during the Scopes "monkey trial." While scientific creationists spin "just-so" stories to support their peculiar version of science, their worldview is consistent and seemingly based on reliable information. Below is how Gary Parker, a former evolutionist, explains his position why scientific creationism should be taught in schools. Parker taught science as a high school teacher and holds advanced degrees in biology and education. He is now a lecturer for the scientific creationist organization *Answers in Genesis*. In a radio interview, Parker was asked, "Has creationism influenced your work as a scientist and as a teacher? Parker's answer was (Parker, n.d.):

> Yes, in many positive ways. Science is based on the assumption of an understandable orderliness in the operation of nature, and the Scriptures guarantee both that order and man's ability to understand it, infusing science with enthusiastic hope and richer meaning. Furthermore, creationists are able to recognize *both* spontaneous *and* created (i.e., internally and externally determined) patterns of order and this opened my eyes to a far greater range of theories and models to deal with the data from such diverse fields as physiology, systematics, and ecology.
>
> Creationism has certainly made the classroom a much more exciting place, both for me and my students...And, of course, on the basic matter of origins, my students and I have the freedom to discuss *both* evolution *and* creation, a freedom tragically denied to most young people today.

The courts have decisively decided creationism cannot be included in school curricula because of its religious origin and purpose. The struggle against scientific creationism will not be over until teachers like Dr. Gary Parker become convinced evolution is a better model. Unless that is done, creationism will enter the classroom eventually. If we applaud teachers for refusing to teach scientific creationism because it is against their conscience and/or their professional ethics to do so, we cannot in the long run force scientific creationists to teach material they similarly reject. Scientific creationists will use the American sense of fair play to argue both sides of the controversy should be presented to students so that they can decide in a mature fashion which model is more convincing. Using a similar strategy, John Peloza filed a suit against his school district on the ground his constitutional rights had been violated because he had taught there was more evidence for an intelligent designer than for evolution. Peloza also claimed that he felt that both evolution and creationism should be discussed in science classes (Sonder, 1999: 93).

Evolutionists have failed to convince a minority of educated, honest persons their anti-evolution position is mistaken. Proponents of creationism will become more convincing until they become successful in including scientific creationism, or more probably intelligent design, in classroom materials.

Scientific creationists have been successful in entering university academic circles; many scientific creationists have earned advanced degrees and have published on secular topics. Henry M. Morris, currently emeritus president of the *Institute for Creation Research* and still prolific scientific creationist author, is also the author of a respected textbook on hydraulic mechanics. Michael Behe is both a molecular biologist and a founder of the modern intelligent design perspective. William A. Dembski, a leader of the intelligent design group, has earned two doctorates (philosophy and mathematics) and masters degrees in statistics and theology. Another leading scientific creationist critic of fossil evidence holds advanced degrees in biology. Scientific creationist Henry M. Morris' book *Men of Science, Men of God* (1998) describes 108 pre-modern scientists who were also creationists in one form or another, including Newton, Faraday, and Kepler. Morris listed eighteen modern creationist scientists, including Werner von Braun, George Washington Carver, and Sir Cecil P. G. Wakeley. Wakeley (1892–1979) was president of the Evolution Protest Movement in England as well as Professor of Surgery and president of the Royal College of Surgeons. The list continues, and Ronald L. Numbers (1992) described the successful academic careers of academics and scientists involved in scientific creationism and its new manifestation of intelligent design.

The scientific creationist *Discovery Institute* in Seattle distributes an anti-evolution document signed by 130 scientists. This document includes the statement that the signatories feel "skepticism toward the Darwinian claim that "random mutation and natural selection account for the complexity of life."" (quote in Holden, 2002) Scientific creationists can now call on a large number of academics willing to support their cause. Morris also notes in his book *Men of Science* that creationism is undergoing a revival, a claim also supported by creationism critic Robert T. Pennock in his *Tower of Babel* (1999). Scientific creationists will no doubt become more visible both in the general society and in academic circles.

On the other hand, the anti-creationist forces are also becoming more active. Those who accept evolution are increasingly disturbed by the charges scientific creationists level against evolutionists, their work, and their textbooks. Eugenie C. Scott, in a review of Jonathan Wells' book *Icons of Evolution* (Wells, 2000), notes that *Icons* has been used as a rationale to attack textbooks containing evolutionary material. *Icons* was used as the basis of a lawsuit against members of the Kanawha County School Board in the state of Arkansas even though *Icons* itself contains factual errors and omits information supporting evolution (Scott, 2001). Evolutionists themselves are becoming better organized to resist scientific creationism and intelligent design.

Public Opinion

A Gallup Organization survey of American adults conducted during 1990 found fifty-five percent opposed replacing the teaching of evolution with creationist material in public schools. A greater proportion, sixty-eight percent, favored the teaching of *both* evolution and creationism. While the higher courts have consistently rejected the arguments scientific creationism and intelligent design are free of religious content, scientific creationists have successfully convinced a large segment of the general public evolution is "only" a theory that has either been disproved or is in a state of crisis. Proof that these views are widespread was illustrated when President Ronald Reagan remarked in a 1980 press conference that, "If it [evolution] is going to be taught, then I think that also the Biblical theory of creation, which is not a theory but the Biblical story of creation, should also be taught." President Reagan used the term "theory" as denoting incomplete knowledge not verified and therefore probably false. Creationists have successfully redefined the concept "theory" in the mind of the public in a manner different from its use by orthodox scientists.

Another Gallup Organization survey of the American adult population took place in November 1991. The respondents were almost equally divided in terms of their acceptance of Young-Earth creationism and theistic evolution. Below are the proportions of Americans giving positive responses to three key questions (U.S. New, & World Report, December 1991: 56ff):

- God created man pretty much in his present form at one time within the last 10,000 years: 47%

- Man has developed over millions of years from less advanced forms of life, but God guided this process, including man's creation: 40%

- Man has developed during one million of year from less developed forms of life. God had no part in this process: 9%

We see from the above roughly half of the American population believe in one or another creationist position. The American population also views the inclusion of both scientific creationism and evolutionary models in schools as fair. The strict evolutionary position of excluding the notion of supernatural involvement in evolutionary processes is rejected by ninety-one percent of the population, placing those who accept naturalistic evolution in the minority. The scientific creationist claim an atheistic educational elite is forcing evolution upon children has merit only if scientific creationists prove evolution is false. Most Americans seem willing to accept both evolution and creationism as curricula material in the spirit of fairness (Morris, 1993: 364). In a 1981 survey of the American population, seventy-six percent of respondents agreed with the statement "Both creation and evolution should be taught."

The Dilemma of Teaching Creationism

Scientific creationists want schools to include their views in high school curricula. This seemingly simple request has potential complications and would result in unanticipated consequences that scientific creationists would reject. Since forty percent of the American public accepts the theistic evolutionary model, creationism in the school may not necessarily reflect the Young-Earth scientific creationist faction. Karen Wiegman has experienced such unanticipated consequences resulting from the introduction of the religious issue in schools. After years of effort, Wiegman convinced members of the Texas Grand Prairie school board to allow her to distribute to students book covers containing the Ten Commandments and Christian messages. (Henderson, 2000: A33 and A34). In response, a member of the Metroplex Atheistic Group demanded equal treatment and was allowed to distribute book covers containing atheistic messages. While Wiegman states she doesn't mind if atheistic or satanic literature is distributed in the schools, most scientific creationists would reject the introduction of overtly atheistic literature in high schools.

At this time any religious and non-religious group can pass out book covers in the Grand Prairie schools as long as the messages are not "disruptive, libelous, obscene, inflammatory, sexually inappropriate for the age of the audience or that endorses action endangering the health or safety of students…" There are a number of other religious and secular groups in Texas whose members may wish to promote their messages in the schools, including anti-abortion groups and witchcraft covens. Should schools be the battleground for such propaganda? The introduction of what courts and others see as religious literature in the schools opens a Pandora box of conflict and misinformation.

What Next?

The one hundred and fifty year controversy between creationists and evolutionists continues and will become more intense as all sides (there are more than two) of the controversy increase their attacks on one other. Pro-evolutionists, who disagree (often intensely) with one another, will feel even more threatened by the attacks of scientific creationists and intelligent designers. The arena for these conflicts will be in large part the struggle over schoolbook and class content. There will also be a continuation of the struggle to limit students to the exposure of evolutionary thought.

The struggle between scientific creationism and evolutionists will also continue as long as scientific creationists believe that evolutionary perspectives threaten their religious beliefs. This conflict will not be settled by new information or the power of logic because the scientific creationists' arguments are beyond reason and logic. Creationists even use hypothetical arguments as if they were correct, as does Ken Ham when he states (Ham, 1993: 18):

> Creationists, of course, would not be surprised if someone found a living dinosaur. However, evolutionists would then have to explain why they made dogmatic statements that man and dinosaur never lived at the same time. I suspect they would say something to the effect that this dinosaur somehow survived because it was trapped in a remote area that has not changed for millions of years. You see, no matter what is found, or how embarrassing it is to evolutionists' ideas, they will always be able to concoct an "answer" because evolution is a belief, it is not science—it is not fact!

Evolutionists are expected to answer hypothetical questions while the presumed answers are assumed to be invalid! Nor is there any acceptance when evolutionists make valid statements supported by well-established research.

Careful analysis of the statements made by scientific creationists indicates creation science in all of its forms is pseudo-science and cannot be accepted as intellectually equal to orthodox sciences using a naturalistic model. Scientific creationists have made, and continue to make, claims that contradict established science. These statements—primarily criticisms of evolutionary knowledge—have been thoroughly discredited. However, the strength (and ultimate weakness) of scientific creationists is not their arguments but in their use of religion to reject or ignore empirical knowledge contradicting their faith.

APPENDIX

Selected Annotated Bibliography

I provide below a list of publications central to the creation/evolution controversy. These books form the core for those who wish to develop an understanding of the major ideas and perspectives in creationism and evolution. Selection necessarily demands that excellent works were excluded, though the following books are among the most rewarding for non-specialists. The list below contains many contemporary "classics" that provide a better understanding of the creation/evolution controversy not possible by reading more specialized works.

Asimov, Isaac (1987) *Beginnings: The Story of Origins—of Life, the Earth, The Universe.* New York: Walker and Company.

> Asimov discusses the beginnings and development of human flight, civilization, various life forms, the moon, the solar system, and the universe. The writing style is informal but clear. Like Stephen Jay Gould, Asimov was one of the most prolific popularizer of scientific and other topics. The chapters on *Homo sapiens*, primates, and mammals are especially good explanations and presentations of evolution.

Aubrey, Frank and William Thwaites (eds.) (1984), *Evolutionists Confront Creationists.* Proceedings of the 63rd Annual Meetings of the Pacific Division, American Association for the Advancement of Science, Volume 1 (part 3): April 30. San Francisco, California: Pacific Division, American Association for the Advancement of Science.

> The Pacific Division of the American association for the Advancement of Science dedicated two sections to the analysis of creationism. Each presenter analyzes creationism from the point of view of his or her specialty. The criticisms of creationism are focused and direct. The authors ignored theological statements while evaluating the testable parts of creationism. Robert V. Gentry presents the creationist perspective on the Young-Earth model of the structure

and age of the universe and the earth. His presentation ends with the conclusion that "*In simpler terms the theory of relativity has been falsified because a major prediction of the theory is now known to be contradicted by an unambiguous experimental result.* Without relativity theory there is no Big Bang, no Hubble relation for the redshift, and no explanation for the CMR in an evolutionary cosmological model (emphasis in the original)." Instead, the center of the universe is a fixed point where God's throne is located as stated in Psalm 103:19. The defense of this position is thoroughly technical though few orthodox physicists would agree with Gentry's conclusions.

Beckwith, Francis J. (2003) *Law, Darwinism, and Public Education: The Establishment Clause and the Challenge of Intelligent Design.* Lanham, Maryland: Rowman & Littlefield Publishers, Inc.

The courts in the last fifteen years have faced the issue of whether intelligent design (ID) should be taught in schools. The author analyzes the issue of scientific creationism and its latest manifestation by focusing on the *Edwards v. Aguillard* 1987 case from analytic and legalistic perspectives in detail. The background information and bibliography are complete and place future court cases dealing with teaching creationism in schools in their proper contexts. The author concludes that ID, even if scientifically acceptable, cannot presently be included as a school topic because of ID's religious nature and origin. The Establishment Clause would prevent the teaching of ID in science courses. However, Beckwith notes that courts could change their definitions of religion to allow the teaching of intelligent design. In addition, the courts could decide ID is a research agenda rather than a religious statement and therefore could logically be included as science material in schools.

Behe, Michael (1996) *Darwin's Black box: The Biochemical Challenge to Evolution.* New York: Simon & Schuster.

Darwin's Black box is the central work of the intelligent design perspective in scientific creationism. Behe claims that evolution is disproved at the biochemical level because organisms display complexities that could not evolve bit by bit. His central concept of *irreducible complexity* advances William Paley's argument by presenting the idea complex biological phenomena cannot operate unless a large number of elements, enzymes, protein, and parts are present at the same time and therefore could not have developed piecemeal in response to evolutionary pressures.

Dawkins, Richard (1996) *The Blind Watchmaker: Why the Evidence of Evolution Reveals a Universe Without Design.* New York: W. W. Norton & Company

Issued originally in 1986, this work is a major work attacking the intelligent design school of creationism by showing how life could have developed without supernatural intervention. Dawkins sees natural selection as a non-random process that has no goals, no purpose, and seems to have goals only through the hindsight of an outside observer. He argues that evolution proceeds through very small changes, most of which are doomed to failure since there are more extinct forms of life than surviving ones. The sections on speciation are clear and follow his general orientation. The work contains a criticism of the punctuated equilibrium theory as proposed by fellow evolutionists Gould and Eldredge.

Eldredge, Niles (2000) *The Triumph of Evolution and the Failure of Creationism.* New York: W. H. Freedom and Company.

The author is a leading paleontologist who developed the concept of punctuated equilibrium with Stephen Jay Gould. Aldredge presents a very strong case that evolution is a workable, testable theory. By contrast, he sees no value in infusing science with religious values as the creationists wish.

He is adamant that evolution has a scientific base. He admits the limits of reliable knowledge dealing with the mechanisms of evolution, and Eldredge acknowledges that studies of the origin of life are inconclusive. However, he does not replace an uncertain attitude with a religious explanation on how life began. The book contains short descriptions of seven important court decisions defining creationism as religious rather than scientific in nature. As expected, Eldredge soundly criticizes the creationists' dismissal of fossil evidence as a reason for their rejection of evolution.

Eve, Raymond E. and Francis B. Harrold (1991) *The Creationist Movement in Modern America.* Boston: Twayne Publications.

The authors analyze creationism as a social movement developing out of Protestant fundamentalism. Unique elements of creationism include its ideological foundations and the search for legitimacy for their beliefs.

The work is an even-handed description of the history of modern creationism, the major values of creationists, and how they have mobilized their resources to protect and propagandize their religious beliefs. There are chapters on what creationists believe and how they are developing new strategies to combat evolution and include creationism in public school curricula. The chapter on creationist organizations is thorough and shows the movement's impressive financial and numerical strength. The last chapter deals with correct predictions of creationists' efforts to make their cause more successful.

Frymire, Philip (2000) *Impeaching Mere Creationism*. San Jose, California: Writers Club Press.

The author devotes his book to criticizing scientific creationist Phillip Johnson. Each chapter deals with a topic covered in Johnson's publications, especially his *Defeating Darwinism by Opening Minds* (1997) and *Darwin on Trial* (1993). Frymire deals in detail with the major points Johnson presents in his criticisms of evolution. He points out the weaknesses of Johnson's arguments and his faulty interpretations of scientific material. The work as a whole is an excellent criticism of scientific creationism.

Gish, Duane T. (1993) *Creation Scientists Answer Their Critics*. El Cajon, California: Institute for Creation Research.

Gish provides detailed analyses of the scientific creationist position by citing the works of creationists and evolutionists finding fault with one or another aspect of evolution. While some topics harmful to creationism are ignored, the work nevertheless is a comprehensive attempt to find weaknesses in the evolution argument. There is no attempt to rely on scripture. Many of the points Gish presents are closely reasoned. The sections on the lack of intermediate fossils and on the laws of thermodynamics are thorough from a creationist perspective.

Gish, Duane T. (1995) *Evolution: The Fossils Still Say No!* El Cajon, California: Institute for Creation Research.

Evolution is a revision of *Evolution: The Challenge of the Fossil Record* (1985) and a continuation of his antievolution arguments in his *Evolution? The Fossils Say No!* (1979 [1972]). Gish presents the Young-Earth scientific creationist argument that evolution is a philosophy rather than a science. He attacks the concepts of geological time and the geologic column (Older fossils and deposits are found below younger fossils and deposits). He then criticizes how evolutionists understand fossil evidence. Gish uses at length evolutionists' criticisms of each other and stresses any ambiguity he finds in the literature to dismiss evolutionary interpretations of speciation and macroevolution. His publications have been dismissed by Stephen Jay Gould and other evolutionists, but they remain very convincing to those who seek a Young-Earth creationist defense. Other creationists have based much of their anti-evolution arguments on Gish's work.

Huse, Scott M. (1997) *The Collapse of Evolution* (third edition). Grand Rapids, Michigan: Baker Books.

Huse, with a doctorate in computer science, focuses on the weaknesses he finds in defenses of evolutionary theory. There is no reliance on Biblical references, making the work a solid example of scientific creationism. The arguments in this book include discussion of gaps in fossil evidence and the mathematically low probability of the emergence of life, though he ignores the positive support for evolution processes. Huse presents criticisms of dating methodologies used by other creationists.

The work contains many examples of the intelligent design perspective by showing the complexity of animal structure and behavior. Page 35 describes the major features of the flight of insects as miraculous rather than the result of evolution. Huse also describes the migratory patterns of birds as too complex to have evolved piecemeal. Appendix B contains an exhaustive list of ninety-eight creationist organizations and their addresses. Appendix D contains two computer programs showing random processes cannot develop complex organisms. These are offered in response to Richard Dawkins' computer program showing random processes can in fact develop complex structures.

Johnson, Phillip E. (1993) *Darwin On Trial* (second edition). Downers Grove, Illinois: InterVarsity Press.

Trained in law and a member of the law faculty at the University of California at Berkeley, Johnson presents a closely reasoned criticism of evolution. The work is one of the most definitive presentations of scientific creationist thought. In chapter nine, he criticizes evolutionary science as non-scientific and based on a number of fallacies and "naturalist" biases. Many of Johnson's criticisms of evolution form the basis of legal defenses to bring creationism into the classroom. Johnson also devotes a chapter to the proposition that evolution is a matter of faith and therefore a religion. The work is especially convincing when Johnson discusses evolution and creationism as equally scientific or as equally matters of faith.

Johnson, Phillip E. (1997) *Defeating Darwinism by Opening Minds*. Downers Grove, Illinois: InterVarsity Press.

Defeating Darwinism is a continuation and popularization of his *Darwin On Trial*. More informal in style, Johnson presents the reasons why evolution is an unproven philosophy. Johnson stresses his central thesis that "scientific materialists have faith that they will eventually find a materialistic theory to explain the origin of life, even though the experimental evidence may be pretty discouraging for now...[The Darwinist] is convinced, on philosophical grounds, that the theory must be true. That's every bit as much of a faith commitment as the belief of a Young-Earth creationist that all radiometric dating must be wrong...(p66)."

McIver, Tom (1992) *Anti-Evolution: A Reader's Guide to Writings Before and After Darwin.* Baltimore and London: The Johns Hopkins University Press.

Originally published in 1988, this remarkable book contains 1,852 citations from the anti-evolution literature. Many of the annotations are so extensive they include not only a summary of the contents of the works cited but also detailed information on earlier editions. Some reviews include quotes as well as who used the material in question.

Milton, Richard (1997) *Shattering the Myths of Darwinism.* Rochester, Vermont: Park Street Press.

Originally published in 1992, *Shattering the Myths* presents arguments for the invalidity of Darwinism and the impossibility of an old earth. Milton deals with the common criticisms made by scientific creationists in a rigorous and comprehensive manner. He covers the often-used arguments made by creationists to defend a young earth and to dismiss geological and fossil evidence contrary to his position. Milton claims Darwinism is declining in acceptance (p. 277) and will soon be replaced by models that conform better to scientific evidence.

Montagu, Ashly, editor, (1984) *Science and Creationism.* Oxford New York: Oxford University Press.

Twenty authors discuss creationism within a scientific framework. The essays form an excellent introduction to the negative aspects of creationism. Each author evaluates creationism in terms of discipline or orientation. Isaac Asimov analyzes the weaknesses of the major arguments of creationism, including:

• Distorting science

• Argument from imperfection

•

- Argument from analogy

- Argument from general consent

Stephen Jay Gould and Robert Root-Berstein evaluate creationism from their separate disciplines. Historian and philosopher Michael Ruse describes his experiences as a witness in the 1981 Arkansas trial that rejected scientific creationism as a science and stated a "balanced" treatment of evolution and creationism was a violation of the U.S. Constitution.

Moreland, J. P. and John Mark Reynolds, editors, (1999) *Three Views on Creation and Evolution.* Grand Rapids, Michigan.

The editors present three creationism models: Young-Earth creationism, Old-Earth creationism, and theistic evolution. Proponents of each theological position defend their beliefs and rationales. A panel of four experts then makes comments on each position. The authors of each view also comment on one another's theologies. The result is a series of well-developed descriptions of the three major creationist theological positions and how their critics evaluate their own and others' theological proposition.

Morris, Henry M. (1976) *The Genesis Record: A Scientific & Devotional Commentary on the Book of Beginnings.* Grand Rapids, Michigan: Baker Book House.

It is difficult to select one or a few publications by Henry Morris to represent the writings of the current leading scientific creationist. Morris has been and continues to be a highly prolific writer. All of his writings are clear and his arguments forcefully presented. There is a tendency to avoid topics that weaken his arguments, but his range of evidence to support scientific creationism is impressive. *The Genesis Record* analyzes the Book of Genesis verse by verse for 668 pages, appendixes, and indexes and is an impressive exposition of his theological position by any standard. There is no attempt to incorporate Biblical higher criticism and each verse is interpreted in a literal manner, though Morris makes common sense interpretations, such as when he states that Genesis 2:4 through Genesis 5:1 "was probably written originally by Adam himself...and in effect represents his own perspective on the creation and first events of human history (p. 83)." Morris states the two accounts of the creation do not contradict each other and the difference in vocabulary indicates a different emphasis rather than that the second passage is a later insertion.

Morris, Henry M., editor, (1985) *Scientific Creationism*. Green Forest, AZ: Master Books.

> There are few works as complete a criticism of Darwinism and naturalistic science as this book. Prepared by the technical staff of the *Institute for Creation Research*, the work is an excellent and imposing example of the best arguments presented by scientific creationists for a young earth, a Genesis flood, and anti-Darwinism. The work defends the scientific creationist position using secular and religious arguments, though they are separated from each other. This work and the one by Richard Milton (see above) are among the best scientific creationists offer.

Morris, Henry M. (1993) *History of Modern Creationism*. Santee, California: Institute for Creation Research.

> A history of scientific creationism from the creationist perspective, this work offers a good description of the attitudes and dedication of creationists. The close ties between creationism and fundamentalist, born-again Protestantism is made clear. There are descriptions of court cases from the scientific creationist point-of-view. The creationists are well organized and dedicated, and have increased in influence during the last few decades. There is a list of creationist organizations throughout the world and their addresses.

Numbers, Ronald L. (1992) *The Creationists: The Evolution of Scientific Creationism*. Berkeley: University of California Press.

> The best available history of twentieth century creationism, this work describes the careers and thoughts of the major supporters of creationism in its many manifestations. Numbers reports on the contents of significant works in addition to the correspondence of creationists. The book is especially informative on the scientific creationists led by Henry M. Morris and his son, John Morris. Numbers describes the development of the *Creation Research Society* and its influence on all creationists. The work not only offers a rich mine of biographical information, but also shows the development and varieties of creationism, primarily in the United States.

Numbers, Ronald L. (1998) *Darwinism comes to America*. Cambridge, Massachusetts: Harvard University Press.

> Evolution became controversial in the United States soon after Darwin's publication of *The Origin of* Species in 1859. After presenting a 150-year review of

the varieties of creationism in the first two chapters, Numbers presents an excellent analysis of the Scopes trial and Darwinism in the South during the 1860s–1920s. There are sections of Adventist, Pentecostal, and American naturalists' reactions to Darwinism. The amount of references is extensive. An appendix offers biographic and bibliographic notes on eighty naturalists who were members of the Natural Academy of Sciences during 1863–1900 with selected statements made by these scientists on evolution.

Pennock, Robert T. (1998) *Tower of Babel: The Evidence Against the New Creationism.* Cambridge, Massachusetts and London, England: The MIT Press.

Trained as a philosopher, Pennock presents one of the most thorough and sophisticated analyses and criticisms of creationism in its various forms. *Tower of Babel* deals with creationist linguistics as a platform from which to criticize creation science. Pennock shows how many creationist beliefs can just as easily defend other non-orthodox beliefs such as a flat earth. The chapters on the evaluation and criticisms of intelligent design and creationism as a science are superior. Two chapters deal with why creationists insist on devoting most of their efforts in criticizing evolution and the potential consequences of allowing scientific creationism in the schools.

Ratzsch, Del (1996) *The Battle of Beginnings: Why Neither Side is Winning the Creation-Evolution Debate.* Downers Grove, Illinois: InterVarsity Press.

In spite of being published by a publishing house that routinely publishes anti-evolution material, this book contains even-handed criticisms of both creationism and evolution, though I personally found the criticisms of creationism the better part of Ratzsch's arguments. A creationist might say the same about the author's criticisms of evolution. The author analyzes the writings of supporters of each side of the controversy. He has a sound knowledge of the literature and he closely analyzes what creationists and evolutionists have published. The criticisms are often very sharp and bound to irritate everyone as he discusses and evaluates all of the major writings in both camps. The lack of an index hinders locating major topics, but the book as a whole is a guide to all of the major relevant issues. Ratzsch is especially good at discovering errors of logic and when authors contradict themselves.

Ridley, Mark, editor, (1997) *Evolution.* New York: Oxford University Press.

Ridley presents selections from a wide variety of journal articles and books dealing with evolution. The selections tend to be short and many are very technical, but together they offer the reader a comprehensive view of all aspects of evolutionary theory, knowledge, and viewpoints. Each section contains a mini essay by the editor placing the following selections in their contexts.

The selections also show the utility of evolutionary theory and knowledge to better understand the variety of organisms. Popularized descriptions of evolutionary topics found elsewhere are easier for the non-specialist to understand because they present over-simplified versions of the material. Ridley's selections show the serious, dedicated side of evolutionary sciences.

Ruse, Michael, editor, (1988) But Is It Science? *The Philosophical Questions in the Creation/Evolution Controversy.* Buffalo, New York: Prometheus Books.

The work is a collection of articles and book chapters containing largely pro-evolution material though there are also a few defenses of creationism, including those by William Paley, Adam Sedgwick, and Duane T. Gish. The emphasis of the work is on philosophical analyses of various aspects of evolutionary models. There are selections dealing with the legal and political controversies of the debate and the work as a whole is a solid introduction to the main features of evolution.

Sarfati, Jonathan (1999) *Refuting Evolution: A Handbook for Students, Parents, and Teachers Countering the Latest Arguments for Evolution.* Green Forest, Arizona: Master Books.

In its eighth printing with more than 200,000 copies in print, this work is a focused criticism of selected aspects of evolution. The author wrote this book with the sponsorship of *Answers in Genesis* as a guide for students and others wishing to develop arguments against evolution. The attacks are specific and there is only one reference to Biblical scripture. All arguments are based on analyses of data or lack of data. The reader can use this work to prepare to argue rationally against evolution. Chapters cover such issues as intelligent design, evolution of whales and birds, missing links, age of the earth, and a criticism of Darwin's concept of natural selection. Although most of the references are from the creationist literature, the arguments presented are convincing from a creationist perspective.

Shermer, Michael (1997) *Why People Believe Weird Things: Pseudoscience, Superstition, and Other Confusions of our Time.* New York: W.H. Freeman and Company.

Although only three chapters deal with creationism, the author presents very concise descriptions and criticisms of creationism. Shermer gives a detailed account of his debate with creationist Duane Gish, and proceeds to present twenty-five creationist arguments/statements and their evolutionist responses. This chapter covers many of the central arguments of scientific creationism and their refutations. The last chapter deals with issues of the nature of science and whether scientific creationism can be considered a science. The author gives space for creationists to present their best arguments. The author is editor of *Skeptic* magazine (skepticmag@aol.com) and offers very cogent evaluations of creationism.

Sonder, Ben (1999) *Evolutionism and Creationism.* Danbury, Connecticut: Franklin Watt.

The author presents both sides of the evolution-creationism arguments. He describes the major elements of the controversy in a concise manner. The presentations form clear and balanced introductions, including a short list of annotated works for further reading. The author focuses in large part on the public debates between creationists and evolutionists, including the Scopes trial and other court cases as well as anti-evolutionary textbook committees. The arguments in this work seem to favor the evolution perspective though Sonder ends his work by suggesting extremists on both sides harm their cause while there is ample room for compromise.

Strahler, Arthur N. (1999) *Science and Earth History: the Evolution/Creation Controversy.* Amherst, New York: Prometheus Books.

There is no more complete or better work comparing the statements scientific creationists have made with findings from orthodox science, especially geology. Strahler begins with a general discussion of science and pseudo-science, the alternative creationist theologies to scientific creationism, then deals with the "scientific" statements of scientific creationism, including the origin of life, the age of the solar system and earth, the impossibility of Genesis-based geology and genetics, and animal and human evolution. Strahler discusses transitional fossils and reptilian transitions with comparisons to the creationist literature on those topics.

Tiffin, Lee (1994) *Creationism's Upside-Down Pyramid: How Science Refutes Fundamentalism.* Amherst, New York: Prometheus Books.

Lee presents the central elements of scientific creationism's arguments dealing with flood geology, the episode of the ark, and animal migration after leaving the ark. These arguments are evaluated and rejected with technical data and logical analysis. There are additional chapters on the creationist challenges to public education, a science-based criticism of creationist statements about the pre-flood vapor canopy, and a critical evaluation of the creationist view of dinosaurs.

Wells, Jonathan (2000) *Icons of Evolution: Science or Myth? Why Much of What We Teach About Evolution is Wrong.* Washington, D.C.: Regnery Publishing, Inc.

The author presents a number of errors and irrelevancies in presentations of support for evolution, including the Miller-Urey Experiments of possible start of life, homology evidence for evolution, changes due to environmental pressures in Darwin's finches, and the pepper moths studies. Wells shows biological textbooks often use incorrect data to support evolution processes. While correct in many instances, he ignores more positive support for evolution, and some of his criticisms are misplaced. He does offer valuable corrections, though he assumes that a few errors indicate the falsity of evolutionary theories. Wells presents convincing criticisms from both the creationist and empirical perspectives for those who wish to reject the existence of evolution.

Whitcomb, John C. (1988) *The World That Perished: An Introduction to Biblical Catastrophism.* Revised edition. Grand Rapids, Michigan: Baker Book House.

One of the founders of modern scientific creationism, Whitcomb's account of the Noachian flood and support for the Young-Earth model was first published in 1960. The work as a result seems less sophisticated than later explanations. Nevertheless, *The World that Perished* contains detailed analyses that support various creationist Biblical passages. Whitcomb emphasizes what he understands to be geological support for a young earth and stresses that the Bible is a good guide to scientific knowledge, especially geology. On page 41, for example, he states that "Psalm 104:8 ["Mountains rose and valleys sank to the levels you decreed"] is actually saying God pushed up great mountain ranges in the continental areas to balance the new depths in the ocean basins."

Whitcomb, John C. and Henry M. Morris (1961) *The Genesis Flood: The Biblical Record and its Scientific Implications*. Phillipsburg, New Jersey: P&R Publishing.

> In its forty-second printing, this work forms the foundation of scientific creationism after George McCready Price's 1935 work on the Genesis flood. The work remains a model of thoroughness. The authors use geological and scriptural information to discuss the nature of Noah's ark, the Genesis flood, and fossil evidence and paleontology. There is no better work to begin to understand the scientific creationists' approach to their subject matter.

Wills, Christopher (1996) *Yellow Fever Black Goddess: The Coevolution of People and Plagues*. Reading, Massachusetts: Helix Books.

> The evolutionary framework explains how protozoa, bacteria, viruses, animals, plants, and humans adapted as they coexisted with one another. Viral enzymes mutate quickly to develop "quasi species" that become immune to vaccines. The AIDS disease had undergone evolution (mutation) since its development in the first baboon and human hosts. The author predicts the emergence of future plagues that will cause great societal changes. The increase in world population and global traveling are creating havoc among minor ecosystems that in turn threaten the viability of major ecologies throughout the world.

Wills, Christopher (1998) *Children of Prometheus: The Accelerating Pace of Human Evolution*. Reading, Massachusetts: Perseus Books.

> Although many examples and case studies in the work are not convincing, the author's thesis is that human evolution has occurred since humanity's separation from other primates. Wills shows that changing physical, geographic, and social environments forced changes in humanity's gene makeup. The book is an interesting and enjoyable analysis of the question whether evolution continues in contemporary times.

About the Author

Jon P. Alston is Professor of Sociology at Texas A&M University. He is the author of seven other books and more than seventy journal articles and book chapters. Dr. Alston received his doctorate in sociology from the University of Texas at Austin. He has taught sociology of religion classes and conducted research on American religious attitudes and values for over twenty years

References

Alston. Jon P. (2002) "Creationism in the Comics," *Reports of the National Center for Science Education* 21 (5–7): 41–43.

Ankerberg, John and John Weldon (1998) *Darwin's Leap of Faith: Exposing the False Religion of Evolution*. Eugene, Oregon: Harvest House Publishers.

Anon. (2000) "*'Monkey Trial' Revisited in Kansas as Evolution Debate Heats Up.*" Houston Chronicle, Friday July 14: 13A (AP release).

Baker, Mace (2003) "Sea Dragons," *Impact* #363 (August): i-iv. Insert in *Acts and Facts* 32 (8).Barbour, Ian G. (2997) *Religion and Science: Historical and Contemporary Issues*. Revised and expanded edition. New York: HarperCollins.

Batten, Don, editor, (200) *The Revised and Extended Answers Book*. Green Forest, Arizona: Master books.

Beckwith, Francis J. (2003) *Law, Darwinism, and Public Education: The Establishment Clause and the Challenge of Intelligent Design*. Lantham, Maryland: Rowman & Littlefield Publisher, Inc.

Behe, Michael J. (1996) *Darwin's Black Box: The Biochemical Challenge to Evolution*. New York: Touchstone.

_____ (2000) "Evidence for Design at the Foundation of Life," pp. 113–29 in Michael J. Behe, William A. Dembski, and Stephen C. Meyer, editors, *Science and Evidence for Design in the Universe*. San Francisco: Ignatius Press.

Berghoef, Gerald and Lester DeKoster (1989) *The Great Divide: Christianity or Evolution*. Grand Rapids, Michigan: The Christian's Library Press.

Berlitz, Charles (1987) *The Lost Ship of Noah: In Search of the Ark at Ararat*. New York: G.P. Putnam's Sons.

Berra, Tim M. (1990) *Evolution and the Myth of Creationism: A basic Guide to the Facts in the Evolution Debate*. Stanford, CA: Stanford University Press.

Birx, H. James (1991) *Interpreting Evolution: Darwin & Teilhard de Chardin*. Buffalo, New York: Prometheus Books.

Bowler, Peter J. (1984) *Evolution: The History of an Idea*. Berkeley, California: University of California Press.

Boxer, Sarah (1987) "Will Creationism Rise Again?" *Discover* (October): 80–5.

Brand, Leonard (1997) *Faith, Reason, & Earth History: A Paradigm of Earth and Biological Origins by Intelligent Design*. Berrein Springs, Michigan: Andrews University Press.

Cairns-Smith, A. Graham (1985) "The First Organisms," *Scientific American* vol. 252 (6): 90–100.

Case-Winters, Anna (2000) "The Argument From Design: What is at Stake Theologically?" *Zygon* 35 (March): 69–81.

Casti, John L. (1989) *Paradigms Lost: Tackling the Unanswered Mysteries of Modern Science*. New York: Avon Books.

Chick, Jack T. (1976) *The Ark*. Chino, California: Chick Publications.

Colbert Edwin H. (1985) *Wandering Lands and Animals: The Story of Continental Drift and Animal Population*. New York: Dover Publications, Inc.

Crapanzano, Vincent (1999) *Serving the Lord: Literalism in America from the Pulpit to the Bench*. New York: New Release.

Custance, Arthur C. (1972 [1959]) *Evolution or Creation?* Grand Rapids, Michigan: Zondervan Publishing House.

Cziko, Gary (1995) *Without Miracles: Universal Selection Theory and the Second Darwinian Revolution*. Cambridge, Massachusetts: The MIT Press.

Darwin, Charles (1958 [1892]) *The Autobiography of Charles Darwin and Selected Letters*. Edited by Francis Darwin. Mineola, NY: Dover Publications, Inc.

_____ (1979 [1859]) *The Origin of Species* (first edition). New York: Gramercy Books.

Davis, Percival and Dan H. Kenyon (1993) *Of Pandas and People: The Central Question of Biological Origins* Second Edition. Dallas, Texas: Haughton Publishing Company.

Dawkins, Richard (1989) "Put Your Money on Evolution," *The New York Times Review of Books* April 9: 34–35.

_____ (1996) *The Blind Watchmaker: Why the Evidence of Evolution Reveals a Universe Without Design.* New York: W. W. Norton & Company.

_____ (1997) *Climbing Mount Improbable.* New York and London: W.W. Norton & Company.

De Camp, L. Sprague (1968*)* *The Great Monkey Trial.* Garden City, New York: Doubleday & Company, Inc.

Dembski, William A. (1999) *Intelligent Design: The Bridge Between Science & Theology.* Downers Grove, Illinois: InterVarsity Press.

_____ (2002) *No Free Lunch: Why Specified Complexity Cannot be Purchased Without Intelligence.* New York: Rowman & Littlefield Publishers.

Denholm, I., G. J. Devine, and M. S. Williamson (2002) "Insecticide Resistance on the Move," *Science* 297 (27 September): 2222–23.

Dennett, Daniel C. (1995) *Darwin's Dangerous Idea: Evolution and the Meanings of Life.* New York: Touchstone.

Desmond, Adrian (1997) *Huxley: From the Devil's Disciple to Evolution's High Priest.* Reading, Massachusetts: Perseus Books.

Dooley, Tom (2003) *the True Story of Noah's Ark.* Green Forest, Arizona: Master books, Inc.

Duve, Christian de (1995) *Vital Dust: The Origin and Evolution of Life on Earth.* New York: BasicBooks.

Edwords, Frederick (1982) "The Dilemma of the Horned Dinosaurs," *Creation/ Evolution* 2 (Summer): 1–11.

Elmendorf, R. G. (1983) "The Voyage of Noah's Ark—An Epilogue," *Creation/ Evolution* 13 (Summer): 39–42.

Eldredge, Niles (2000) *The Triumph of Evolution and the Failure of Creationism.* New York: W.H. Freeman and Company.

Eve, Raymond and Francis B. Harrold (1991) *The Creationist Movement in Modern America.* Boston: Twayne Publishers.

Ferguson, C. W. (1968) "Bristlecone Pines: Science and Aesthetics," *Science* 159 (February): 839–46.

Forrest, Barbara (2001) "The Wedge at Work," pp. 5–53 in Robert T. Pennock, editor, *Intelligent Design Creationism and Its Critics: Philosophical, Theological, and Scientific Perspectives.* Cambridge: The MIT Press.

Frair, Wayne and Percival Davis (1994) *A Case for Creation* (third edition). Lewisville, Texas: Accelerated Christian Education, Inc.

Franzen, Hugo F. (1983) "Thermodynamics: The Red Herring," Pp 127–135 in David B. Wilson (ed.), *Did The Devil Make Darwin Do It?* Ames, Iowa: The Iowa State University Press.

Fry, C. George and Jon Paul Fry (1989) *Pioneering a Theology of Evolution: Washington Gladden and Pierre Teilhard de Chardin.* Lanham, New York: University Press of America.

Frymire, Philip (2000) *Impeaching Mere Christianity.* New York: Writers Club Press.

Galusha, Walter T. (1964) *Fossils and the Word of God.* New York: Exposition Press.

Gibson, Joyce L. (1999) *Genesis: God's Word for the Biblically-Inept.* Lancaster, PA: Starburst Publishers.

Gilchrist, George W. (1997) "The Elusive Scientific Basis of Intelligent Design Theory," *Reports of the National Center for Science Education* 17 (May/June): 14–5.

Ginger, Rau (1958) *Six Days or Forever? Tennessee v. John Thomas Scopes.* Boston, Massachusetts: Beacon Press.

Gish, Duane T. (1978) *The Fossils Say No!* San Diego, California: Creation-Life Publishers.

_____ (1993) *Creation Scientists Answer Their Critics.* El Cajon, California: Institute for Creation Research.

_____ (1995) *Evolution: The Fossils Still Say No!* El Cajon, California: Institute for Creation Research.

Glanz, James (2001) "Intelligent-Design Theory Gains as Newest Idea on Life's Origins," *Houston Chronicle* (April 8): 14A.

Godfrey, Laurie R. (1981) "An Analysis of the Creationist Film, "Footprints in Stone."" *Creation/Evolution* 6 (Fall): 23–30.

_____, editor, (1983) *Scientists Confront Creationism.* New York: W.W. Norton & Company.

Gough, J. B. (1983) "The Supposedly Dichotomy Between Creationism and Evolution," *Creation/Evolution* 12 (Spring): 26–31.

Gould, Stephen Jay (1981) *The Mismeasure of Man.* New York: W.W. Norton & Company.

_____ (1983) *Hen's Teeth and Horse's Toes.* New York: W.W. Horton & Company.

_____ (1995) *Dinosaur in a Haystack: Reflections in Natural Science.* New York: Harmony Books.

_____ (1997) "Nonoverlapping Magisteria," *Natural History* 106 (March): 16–22 and 60–2.

Grant, Bruce S. (2002) "Sour Grapes of Wrath," *Science* 297 (9 August): 940–41.

Hall, E. Raymond (1981) *The Mammals of North America.* New York: John Wiley and Sons.

Ham, Ken (1987) *The Lie: Evolution.* Colorado Springs, Colorado: Master Books.

_____ (1993) *Dinosaurs and the Bible?* Florence, Kentucky: Answers in Genesis.

_____ (1999) *Did Adam have a bellybutton? And Other Tough Questions About the Bible.* Green Forest, Arizona: Master Books.

_____ (2001) *Dinosaurs of Eden: A Biblical Journey through Time.* Green Forest, Arizona: Master Books, Inc.

_____ (2003) "The True Story of Noah's Ark." *Answers Update* 10 (7): 1–2.

_____ and Mark Dinsmore (1997) *Amazing Bible Facts About Noah's Ark.* Port Deposit, Maryland: Wellspring Publishing Company.

Hartshorne, Charles (1970) "Deity as the Inclusive Transcendence," Pp. 155–160 in George N. Shuster and Ralph E. Thorson, editors, *Evolution in Perspective: Commentaries in Honor of Pierre Lecomte du Noüy.* Notre Dame, ID: University of Notre Dame Press.

Henderson, Jim (2000) "No Cover-Up: Religious, Atheistic Material OK at Schools," *Houston Chronicle* August 26: A33, A34.

Hendry, Andrew P., John K. Wenburg, et al. (2000) "Rapid Evolution of Reproductive Isolation in the Wild: Evidence from Introduced Salmon," *Science* 290 (20 October): 516–8.

Hitch, Charles J. (1982) "Dendrochronology and Serendipity," *American Scientist* 70 (3): 300–5.

Holden, Constance (2002) "Georgia County Opens door to Creationism," *Science* 298 (4 October): 35–36.

Hovind, Kent E. (n.d.) *"Creation Seminar Series Part 3"* (Video). Pensacola, Florida: Creation Science Evangelism

Huse, Scott M. (1997) *The Collapse of Evolution* (third edition). Grand Rapids, Michigan: Baker Books.

Irvine, William (1955) *Apes, Angels, and Victorians.* Cleveland and New York: The World Publishing Company.

Johanson, Donald and James Shreeve, (1989) *Lucy's Child: The Discovery of a Human Ancestor.* New York: William Morrow and Company, Inc.

Johnson, Phillip E. (1991) *Darwin On Trial.* Downers Grove, Illinois: InterVarsity Press.

Kerr, Richard A (2000). "Ice, Mud Point to CO_2 in Glacier Cycle," *Science* 289 (15 November: 1868): 1868.

Kinstisch, Eli (2001) "Is Life That Simple?" *Discover* 22 (4): 66–71.

Kitcher, Philip (1982) *Abusing Science: The Case against Creationism.* Cambridge, Massachusetts: The MIT Press.

_____ (2001) "Born-Again Creationism," pp. 257–287 in Robert T. Pennock, editor, *Intelligent Design Creationism and Its Critics: Philosophical, Theological, and Scientific Perspectives.* Cambridge: The MIT Press.

Kofahl, Robert E. (1981) "The Bombardier Beetle shoots Back," *Creation/Evolution* 5 (Summer): 12–14.

Krogman, M. Wilton (1951) "The Scars of Human Evolution," *Scientific American* Volume 185 (December): 54–7.

Kuhn, Thomas S. (1970) *The Structure of Scientific Revolutions* Revised edition. Chicago: The University of Chicago Press.

Larson, Edward J. (1989) *Trial and Error: The American Controversy Over Creation and Evolution* (updated edition). New York: Oxford University Press.

Levine, Laurence W. (1965) *Defender of the Faith: William Jennings Bryan, The Last Decade 1915–1925.* New York: Oxford University Press.

Lietha, Dan and Stacia Byers (2000) "Answers for Kids #9," *Creation Ex Nihilo* 22 (4): 36–9.

Lindsell, Harold (1976) *The Battle for the Bible*. Grand Rapids, MI: Zondervan.

Livingstone, David D. (1987) *Darwin's Forgotten Defenders: The Encounter Between Evangelical Theology and Evolutionary Thought*. Grand Rapids, Michigan: Wm. B. Eerdmans Publishing Co.

Lynch, Michael and John S. Conery (2000) "The Evolutionary Fate and Consequences of Duplicated Genes," *Science* 290 (10 November): 1151–55.

Marlow, Jeremy R., Carina B. Lange, Gerold Wefer, and Antoni Rossill-Melé (2000) "Upwelling Intensification as Part of the Pliocene-Pleistocene Climate Transition," *Science* 290 (22 December): 2288–291.

Marsden, George M. (1980) *Fundamentalism and American Culture: The Shaping of Twentieth-Century Evangelicalism: 1870–1925*. New York: Oxford University Press.

Maslin, Mark A. and Stephen J. Burns (2000) "Reconstruction of the Amazon Basin Effective Moisture Availability Over the Past 14,000 Years," *Science* 290 (22 December): 2285–287.

Mayle, Francis E., Rachel Burnbridge and Timothy J. Killeen (2000) "Millennial-Scale Dynamics of Southern Amazonian Rain Forests," *Science* 290 (22 December): 2291–294.

McGowan, Chris (1984) *In the Beginning: A Scientist Shows Why the Creationists Are Wrong*. Buffalo, New York: Prometheus Books.

McIver, Tom (1988) "Formless and Void: Gap Theory Creationism." *Creation/Evolution* 8 (Fall): 1–24.

Miller, Kenneth R. (1999) *Finding Darwin's God: A Scientist's Search for Common Ground Between God and Evolution*. New York: Cliff Street Books.

Miller, Richard (1987) *Fact and Method: Explanation, Confirmation and Reality in the Natural and Social Science*. Princeton, New Jersey: Princeton University Press.

Moore, Robert A (1981) "Arkeology: A New Science in Support of Creation:" *Creation/Evolution* 6 (Fall): 6–15.

_____ (1983) "The Impossible Voyage of Noah's Ark," *Creation/Evolution* 11 (Winter): 1–43.

Morris, Henry M. (1966) *Studies in the Bible and Science or Christ and Creation.* Philadelphia, Pennsylvania: Presbyterian and Reformed Publishing Co.

_____ (1972) *The Remarkable Birth of Planet Earth.* Minneapolis: Dimension.

_____ (1976) *The Genesis Record: A Scientific & Devotional Commentary on the Book of Beginnings.* Grand Rapids, Michigan: Baker Book House.

_____ (1977a [1965]) *The Beginning of the World.* Denver, Colorado: Accent Books.

_____ (1977b) *The Scientific Case for Creation.* San Diego, CA: Creation-Life Publishers, Inc.

_____ (1984) *The Biblical Basis for Modern Science.* Grand Rapids, MI: Baker Book.

_____ (1985) *Scientific Creationism.* Green Forest, Arizona: Master Books.

_____ (1989) *The Long War Against God: The History and Impact of the Creation/Evolution Conflict.* Grand Rapids, MI: Baker book House.

_____ (1993) *History of Modern Creationism.* second edition. Santee, California: Institute for Creation research.

_____ (1998) *Men of Science—Men of God: Great Scientists of the Past Who Believed the Bible.* El Cajon, California: Master Books.

_____, editor, (1985) *Scientific Creationism.* Green Forest, Arizona: Master Books.

_____ (2000) *Biblical Creationism: What Each Book of the Bible Teaches About Creation and the Flood.* Green Forest, Arizona Master books.

_____ and John D. Morris (1996) *The Modern Creation Trilogy. Volume One*. Green Forest, Arizona: Master Books.

_____ (2003) "Evolutionists and the Moth Myth," *Back to Genesis* No. 176 insert in *Acts and Facts* volume 32 (8): a-c.

Morris, John D. (1994) *Noah's Ark and the Ararat Adventure*. Green Forest, Arizona: Master Books.

_____ and Ken Ham (1990) *What Really Happened to the Dinosaurs?* Green Forest, Arizona: Master Books.

Morris, Simon Conway (1998) *The Crucible of Creation: The Burgess Shale and the Rise of Animals*. New York: Oxford University Press.

Nelson, Paul and John Mark Reynolds (1999) Pp 39–75 in J. P. Moreland and John Mark Reynolds (eds.) *Three Views on Creation and Evolution*. Grand Rapids, Michigan: Zondervan Publishing House.

Numbers, Ronald, L. (1992) *The Creationists: The Evolution of Scientific Creationism*. Berkeley and Los Angeles: University of California Press.

_____ (1998) *Darwinism Comes to America*. Cambridge: Harvard University Press.Oard, Michael J (1990) "A New Discovery of Dinosaur Eggs and Embryos in West-Central Argentina," *Creation Ex Nihilo Technical Journal* 13 (2): 3–4.

_____ (2003) "Are Polar Ice Sheets Only 4500 Years Old?" *Impact* 361 (July): i-iv. [Insert in *Acts and Facts* 32 (July, 2003)]

Olshansky, S. Jay, Bruce A. Carnes, and Robert N. Butler (2001) "If Humans Were Built to Last," *Scientific American* 284 (March): 50–5.

Overman, Dean L. (1997) *A Case Against Accident and Self-Organization*. New York: Rowman & Littlefield.

Paley, William (1900 [1802]) *Natural Theology*. New York: American Tract Society.

Parker, Gary (n.d.) *From Evolution to Creation: A Personal Testimony*. Florence, Kentucky: Answers In Genesis.

Patterson, Colin (1999) *Evolution* second edition. Ithaca, New York: Cornell University Press.

Pennisi, Elizabeth (2000) "Twinned Genes Live Life in the Fast Lane," *Science* 290 (10 November): 1065–6.

Pennock, Robert T. (1999) *Tower of Babel: The Evidence Against the New Creationism.* Cambridge, Massachusetts: The MIT Press.

Perloff, James (1999) *Tornado in a Junkyard: The Relentless Myth of Darwinism.* Arlington, Massachusetts: Refuge Books.

Price, George McCready (1935) *The Modern Flood Theory of Geology.* New York: Fleming H. Revell Company.

Ratzsch, Del (1996) *The Battle of Beginnings: Why Neither Side is Winning the Creation-Evolution Debate.* Downers Grove, Illinois: InterVarsity Press.

Raup, David (1983) "The Geological and Paleontological Arguments of Creationism," pp. 147–62 in Laurie R. Godfrey, editor, *Scientists Confront Creationism.* New York: W. W. Horton and Co.

Rice, Stanley (1988) "Scientific Creationism: Adding Imagination to Scripture," *Creation/Evolution* 14 (Fall): 25–36.

Rich, Patricia Vickers, Thomas Hewitt Rich, Mildred Adams Fenton and Carroll Lane Fenton (1996) *The Fossil Book: A record of Prehistoric Life.* Mineola, New York: Dover Publications, Inc.

Ridley, Mark (1985) *The Problems of Evolution.* Oxford, England: Oxford University Press.

_____, editor, (1997) *Evolution.* New York: Oxford University Press.

Ross, Hugh (1998) *The Genesis Question: Scientific Advances and the Accuracy of Genesis.* Colorado Springs, Colorado: Navpress.

Ruse, Michael (1982) *Darwinism Defended: A Guide to the Evolution Controversies.* Menlo Park, California: The Benjamin/Cummings Publishing Company, Inc.

_____ (1998) *Taking Darwin Seriously: A Naturalistic approach to Philosophy*. Amherst: Prometheus books.

_____ (1999) *Mystery of Mysteries: Is Evolution a Social Construction?* Cambridge: Harvard University Press.

_____ (2003) *Darwin and Design: Does Evolution Have a Purpose?* Cambridge: Harvard University Press.

Sarfati, Jonathan (2003) "Can It Bee?" *Creation* 25 (March-July): 44–45.

Savoye, Craig (2000) "Whose 'Science?'" *The Christian Science Monitor*. July 2.

Schadewald, Robert J. (1982) "Six 'Flood' Arguments Creationists Can't Answer," *Creation/Evolution* (Summer): 12–7.

_____ (1983) "Letter to the Editor," *Creation/Evolution* 13 (Summer): 48–9.

Schönknecht, Gerhard and Siegfried Scherer (1997) "Too Much Coal for a Young Earth? *Creation Ex Nihilo Technical Journal* 11 (part 3): 278–82

Scott, Eugenie (2001) "Fatally Flawed Iconoclasm," *Science* 292 (22 June): 2257–258.

Segraves, Kelly L. (1975) *Sons of God Return*. Old Tappan, New Jersey: Fleming H. Revell Company.

Shermer, Michael (1997) *Why People Believe Weird Things: Pseudoscience, Superstition, and Other Confusions of Our Time*. New York: W. H. Freeman and Company.

Shipman, Pat (1998) *Archaeopteryx and the Evolution of Bird Flight*. New York: Simon & Schuster.

Skokstad, Eric (2000) "Hominid Ancestor May have Knuckle Walked," *Science* 287 (24 March): 2131–2.

Smith, John Maynard (1975) *The Theory of Evolution*. Cambridge, England: Cambridge University Press.

Smout, Kary Doyle (1998) *The Creation/Evolution Controversy: A Battle for Cultural Power*. Westport, Connecticut: Praeger.

Sonder, Ben (1999) *Evolution and Creationism*. Danbury, Connecticut: Franklin Watts.

Spetner, Lee (1998) *Not By Chance! Shattering the Modern theory of Evolution*. Brooklyn, New York: The Judaica Press, Inc.

Stokstad, Erik (2001) "Exquisite Chinese Fossils Add New Pages to Book of Life," *Science* 291 (12 January): 232–6.

Strahler, Arthur N. (1999) *Science and Earth History: The Evolution/Creation Controversy*. Buffalo New York: Prometheus Books.

Tattersall, Ian (1998) *Becoming Human: Evolution and Human Uniqueness*. New York: Harcourt Brace & Company.

Thompson, Bruce, editor, (2003) *Evolution: Fact or Fiction?* Farmington Hills, MI: Greenhaven Press.

Thompson, John B. (1990) *Ideology and Modern Culture: Critical Social Theory in the Era of Mass Communication*. Stanford, California: Stanford University Press.

Thorndike, Jonathan L. (1999) *Epperson v. Arkansas: The Evolution-Creationism Debate*. Berkeley Heights, New Jersey: Enslow Publishers, Inc.

Tiffin, Lee (1994) *Creationism's Upside-Down Pyramid: How Science Refutes Fundamentalism*. Amherst, New York: Prometheus Books.

Van Till, Howard J. (2001) "The Creation: Intelligently Designed or Optimally Equipped?" pp. 486–512 in Robert T. Pennock, editor, *Intelligent Design Creationism and its Critics: Philosophical, Theological, and Scientific Perspectives*. Cambridge: The MIT Press.

Wade, Nicholas, editor, (1998) *The Science Times Book of Fossil and Evolution*. New York: The Lyons Press.

Ward, Peter D. and Donald Brownlee (2000) *Rare Earth: Why Complex Life is Uncommon in the Universe*. New York: Copernicus.

Watch Tower Bible & Tract Society of Pennsylvania (1967) *Did Man Get Here by Evolution or by Creation?* Brooklyn, New York: Watchtower Bible and Tract Society of New York, Inc.

_____ (1998) *Is There a Creator Who Cares About You?* Brooklyn, New York: Watchtower Bible and Tract society of New York, Inc.

Webb, George E. (1994) *The Evolution Controversy in America.* Lexington, Kentucky: The University Press of Kentucky.

Weber, Christopher Gregory (1980) "The Bombadier Beetle Myth Exploded," *Creation/Evolution* 3 (Winter): 1–5.

_____ (1981) "Response to Dr. Kofahl," *Creation/Evolution* 5 (Summer): 15–7.

Weiner, Jonathan (1995) *The Beak of the Finch: A Story of Evolution in Our Time.* New York: Vintage Books.

Wells, Jonathan (2000) *Icons of Evolution: Science or Myth? Why Much of What We Teach About Evolution is Wrong.* Washington, D. C. Regnery Publishing, Inc.

Whitcomb, John C. (1988) *The World That Perished.* Grand Rapids, Michigan: Baker Book House.

_____ and Henry M. Morris (1961) *The Genesis Flood: The Biblical Record and its Scientific implications.* Phillipsburg, New Jersey: Presbyterian and Reformed Publishing Company.

Wieland, Carl (2003) "Fighting for Mussolini," *Creation* 25 (March-May): 32–33.

Wilford, John Noble (2001) "Feathered Fossil Find Backs Dino-Bird Link," *Houston Chronicle* April 26: 21A.

Wise, Kurt P. (2002) *Faith, Form, and Time: What the Bible Teaches and Science Confirms about Creation and the Age of the Universe.* Nashville, Tennessee: Broadman & Holman Publishers.

Witham, Larry, A. (2002) *Where Darwin Meets the Bible: Creationists and Evolutionists in America*. New York: Oxford University Press.

Wolfram, Stephen (2002) *A New Kind of Science*. Champaign, Illinois: Wolfram Media.

Woodmorappe, John (1996) *Noah's Ark: A Feasibility Study*. Santee, California: Institute for Creation Research.

_____, editor, (1999) *Studies in Flood Geology: A Compilation of Research studies Supporting Creation and the Flood*. El Cajon, California: Institute for Creation Research.

_____ (2000) "Hypercanes: Rainfall Generators During the Flood?" *Creation Ex Nihilo Technical Journal* 14 (2): 123–127.

Zhang, Fucheng and Zhonghe Zhou (2000) "A Primitive Enantiornithine Bird and the Origin of Feathers," *Science* 290 (December): 1955–8.

Zimmer, Carl (2000) "The Hidden Unity of Hearts," *Natural History* 109 (April): 56–65.

Index

0-595-29108-2

Printed in the United States
21254LVS00004B/292